DO IT (Then Talk About It)

DO IT

(Then Talk About It)

An Autobiography by
Troy E. Scoughton

ISBN: 979-8-9898971-4-8

Cover design and formatting by Borderlands Media.

First edition 2024

Published by Borderlands Media
275 W Farney LN
Las Cruces, NM 88005

https://www.borderlandsmedia.com/

Dedication

*To my lovely wife Sylvia, who promises me
my next home office will have a door.*

Table of Contents

The Army's the best thing that ever happened to her

Sarah really didn't know what she wanted to do after high school. Wetumpka was a beautiful small town, but was without a lot of opportunities. All she knew for certain is that she didn't want to spend the rest of her life working as a checkout girl at Publix.

When the Army recruiter came to her school, she went to see him and signed up for the test- simply out of curiosity. Why not? A few days later she was surprised to get a call, and went into the recruitment center that weekend. She had aptitude for electronics and could sign up for just about any school she wanted. Who would've guessed?

Explosive Ordnance Disposal at Fort Lee Virginia was one of the hardest to go through, apparently- so that was the one she picked; go big or go home. She went home and talked it over with her parents, and signed up that afternoon.

After graduation in 1997 from Wetumpka High School, she went to basic training and 8 tough weeks later found herself at Ft. Lee, learning all there was to know about disarming bombs. It was the coolest thing she had ever done, and sixteen weeks later she was awarded the MOS of 89D and got promoted.

Six years later, she found herself in a combat deployment in Iraq; recently married, re-upped for another three years in the Army, and a newly pinned Staff Sergeant in charge of her own squad. Similarly, her new husband was a Staff Sergeant, too. Life was good.

Today was work as usual, and, as with every mission, you had to be careful. First, you ensure the area is clear; if the worst happens, we don't need a bunch of bystanders getting hurt. Second, give it some time- only fools rush in. Third, find the detonation wire(s) going to the bomb, and cut them.

She had uncovered a couple of clever detonation schemes herself. That included one from a month prior, where the bomber had the blasting cap wired to two nails right next to his back door spaced just the right distance for a 9V battery to be touched as he ran from his house. Ingenious but deadly, her team found it before he could use it. That day they disarmed the bomb and caught the bomber; a textbook perfect mission.

That was then- now, things didn't seem much different in regards to success. The area was cleared, the wires were cut, and lots of time had passed. Most of the bystanders had already gotten bored and gone home, but she was alert-ready. Outfitted in a heavy bomb suit, she approached the bomb. It was hot, probably over 100 degrees, but that was the job and she felt safe in the heavy, immobile, bombproof suit.

As she approached, she saw the bomb was nothing new. Three surplus 155 artillery rounds, stuffed with cheap (but effective) electric detonators. Wires (now cut) ran off in the direction of a house a few hundred meters away. All the bomber had to do was touch the wires to a battery (probably in his house) and the bomb would explode. But those wires had been cut, and those bombers, arrested.

She always found it almost comical how Hollywood always-depicted bombs with complicated timers counting down or at least beeping and flashing red lights. She had never seen any of those and imagined the bomb builders didn't get to see many of those movies.

_______________ *EOD in Bomb Suit* _______________

She began to talk herself through the process again. Step one, make sure you're safe. Step two, make the bomb safe. She reached in to pull the detonators out of the top artillery round, just as she had done a million times before.

But this time was different. At that second, the radio signal was sent from a hidden bomber with a $10 RC car controller bought last week at an outdoor market in town. The 27 MHz radio signal, the most common signal available for radio-controlled cars, was received at the bomb. This receiver was modified and no longer controlled the tires of a child's toy, but instead detonated a bomb. The receiver connected the remote battery power to the blasting caps in a few milliseconds, and within the blink of an eye, the bomb exploded.

It was massive, and Sarah's bomb proof suit offered little protection as all three artillery rounds went off simultaneously. She was thrown into the air and landed thirty feet away from the bomb in the direction of her team. She was literally crushed by the force of the explosion- ripped open by the shell casings, nails, and all the other shrapnel taped to the outside of the shells. Heroic attempts to revive SSG Helms had no effect. She was evacuated to the rear area; her husband and family were notified, her remains returned to Dover and later buried back in Wetumpka. She was the casualty of the new generation of remote detonated bombs that would later become known as IEDs.

In the weeks and months that followed, many of these devices were manufactured and detonated: causing, over the duration of this war, half of the casualties and injuries sustained in total.

Chapter One

The wedding was a formal one; her daddy had a white shotgun

I was born in February of 1956 in Orlando, Florida. Now, before you get too excited about the number one vacation destination in the world, you must realize that when I was a kid, Orlando was little more than a crossroads. I-75 came in from the north to Miami and I-4 (east and west) connected Tampa (on the Gulf Coast) and Daytona Beach (on the Atlantic side). We were also home of Orlando Air Force Base until they closed in the 70's. Later was when we became home of Walt Disney World- but that was after my time there.

My mom Nancy and dad Bert met in the spring of 1955 - probably in Orlando - and I can't imagine how it happened, but my mom got pregnant about the middle of May. My step-granddad was a Deputy Sheriff and I can believe that my mom being two months pregnant due to some airman from the base did make him overly happy, at the time. They were married on July 24th of 1955, and I was born on February 15th the next year. As I understand it, I was named after a friend of my dad's and given his middle - and last - name, so: Troy Eugene Scoughton.

I only remember a few events from early childhood. While my dad was stationed in Texas, I remember playing with Horned Lizards; I think we called them horny toads. Then one day while at that same base, I got curious and stuck a fork in the wall socket, what a surprise that was. I later became an Electrical Engineer and believe my early experiments with electricity may be the reason. During that same period I confessed my love for the little girl next door by taping a sign to the window in our front door- I'm still waiting for her reply.

I think we went back to Florida when my dad got sent to Turkey for a couple of years in the early 60's. While he was gone my mom took me to an air show at the local air base. It must have been tough because by then my little brother Clark, 2 years younger, was on the scene, so mom had her hands full, and I escaped. She panicked.

I understand she (and by then the Air Police) spent over an hour trying to find this curious four-year-old in the middle of this huge crowd. She finally located me sitting in the cockpit of a jet fighter asking dozens of questions. I never flew in the front seat of a military aircraft but spent many hours in the back.

When dad came back from overseas, he and my mom didn't stay married very long. I always blamed my mom, being a bit of a party girl, but doing research for this book, I discovered that on the heels of his divorce from my mom, my dad married another woman (who he also divorced a few years later).

Either way, I didn't speak to my father again until I was in my forties. Not really my decision - his. I guess he owed my mom back alimony and avoided us for many years. We became friends later in life, just before he died, and I am glad we did. Wish we had had more time, and wish he could have met his grandkids. He spoke to them on the phone but they never met in person. You never know how much time you have – I better get busy finishing this book.

After my mom and dad got divorced, we lived next to my Grandparents for a while in a rented house. My Grandma? The sweetest woman that ever lived. She always made a big dinner on Sundays so we could all eat together, and always had ice cream in her freezer. Just before my father left, my grandmother had us all over for Sunday dinner (my dad included). You know what I remember? My Dad would not eat rice. The story I heard was that he was a Prisoner of War in Korea and was fed only rice. After getting out of that prison he never ate rice again … and you know what? Every dish my grandmother served that Sunday contained rice - even dessert.

My dad got the hint and left, and I didn't see him again for 40 years. Guess my dad had to stop for a burger on his way out of town.

———————————— *My Dad* ————————————

My step-grandfather, the only male in my life during my childhood, was a bit of a hard-ass. He'd been the Sheriff of Orange County, so I guess he had to be. I pulled some real bone headed stuff with my grandpa. I was always stealing his hidden playboys and sneaking across the street into the local orange grove to look at the pictures. I think I might have been only in third grade and I'm sure I had no idea what I was looking at, but I liked it enough to keep getting in trouble for 'em.

Other than that? Well, I was always making stuff. I found an old doorknob in his shop and figured out how to take it apart, put it back together; how it worked. I took it to show-and-tell at the beginning of the second grade and my teacher was sure I was a genius.

Later I made an electric chair for roaches with half of the electrical circuit on one set of fingers and the other on a second set. I caught a couple of roaches (not hard to do in central Florida) and threw them into the roach electric chair for the big test. My new invention had no effect on the roaches, though … they just crawled off.

I went on to something else, forgot about the roach electric chair and left it plugged in. When my grandpa went out to his shop to clean up my mess, he got the shock of his life. I sure heard about that later.

My mom bought a house in Wethersfield; a large sub-division in Altamonte Springs, FL, and we moved in not long after. I was seven and, honestly, it was great. My teacher thought I was a genius (after the door lock at show and tell) and taught us all to sing "Fire and Rain" by James Taylor (I still know all the words). There were lots of kids our age there and the guy across the street tried to teach me archery and how to bow hunt. I shot a squirrel and cooked it. It was the toughest thing I ever tried to eat. I never shot another.

Not everything was perfect, but I can't remember much that wasn't.

Wethersfield

My mom loved to make ceramics and she even had a small kiln in the utility shed (don't touch it, it gets hot!) and I had a tent in the backyard (to play doctor with local girls my age) and went to just about every church you could imagine. The vacation bible school buses would come through our neighborhood and pick us up. I went to all of them. The kids down the street were Seventh Day Adventist. I really didn't know what that meant at the time, but I knew they couldn't watch cartoons on Saturday morning. Are you kidding?

What else was there to live for at seven? For all the sacrifice those kids made (no cartoons on Saturday morning!), the older one still made it down to my tent to play doctor.

There was one television program that was the most important. It was not on Saturday morning, it was on Wednesday evening. You knew when it was on because it was always "The Same Bat Time, Same Bat Channel" - yes, it was Batman. The kid behind me had a color TV (can you believe it?) and I'm sure that kid's parents got to hate Wednesday evenings, because I was there and we were watching Batman - (WHAM!, POW!, BIFF!)- and in color!

Then as quickly as it started, it ended. My mom told us we were moving. She told us it was because she forgot to file "Homestead Exemption" (something to do with a tax exemption) but honestly I just think we were right on the edge of making it, my dad stopped paying child support (he got remarried) and my mom got pregnant. Our fragile situation quickly came apart ... so we moved to a place that a single mom in Orlando could afford.

Chapter Two

Reeves Terrace, Orlando

We had to move to the one place where an unmarried pregnant mother with two kids, a minimum wage job, and no child support could manage to live in Orlando: the projects. We weren't alone; the place was filled with unwed mothers and their unsupported kids.

Reeves Terrace is right in the middle of town and our first place was in the 'The Old Terrace'. Mostly two-story duplexes- probably old military housing- but it was okay. There was a Boy's Club across the street, and we would go there every day after school until my mom got home from work. I learned how to shoot pool, box a little, played basketball, and even learned how to play chess. I loved the Boy's Club.

———————————— *Old Terrace* ————————————

I'm sure we barely made ends meet, but that was by design. Your rent was based on your ability to pay. So, if mom got a raise or worked two jobs, they raised our rent. That way they keep you where you belong: at the bottom. We didn't know any better, though, and I think we were happy. It was (probably still is) a damn tough system to escape. A lot of single moms and kids there. Most stayed a long time. It was very easy to get in there- still, hard to leave.

I believe today that there are many entitled people that would like to see the whole country this way. Might look good from the balcony of their big houses on the hill; not so much from the tiny houses inside of the projects.

Right down the end of the block was a small store and behind that the Boys Club. There was also a ball field and a big empty field behind that, where I could launch rockets. I loved to make model rockets. They were cool! There were some that could take pictures, but those were a little out of my league (and price range). A boy could dream.

I entered a contest at the Colonial Photo and Hobby (it's still there today on Colonial and Mills). I built a rocket with windows and passengers (wanted it to look like a commercial airliner), and I won the contest. Now, I did have all my buddies' vote for me every time they went to the hobby shop… ,so maybe it was fixed, … but I won a huge Saturn V model rocket. It took a 'D' motor (that was a big one). I built it, and it looked just like the rocket that went to the moon. I finished it, launched it, it went up 100 feet or so, and then … came back to earth under full power. Nothing much was left of it after impact.

In a few years we moved to the 'New Terrace'. Sounds the same- allow me to explain the difference. The only access to Reeves Terrace was from South Street: a good-sized multi-lane, one way street. So, if us kids were going to raise hell, we'd go into the Old Terrace and start yelling, throwing old bike tires on peoples' roofs. You know, juvenile delinquent stuff. Somebody usually called the police pretty fast. When the cops arrived in the Old Terrace to restore order, we would run to the New Terrace. The cops wouldn't get out of their cars and walk across the Terrace at night, so they would head back up South Street and loop back on Anderson (the one way street going the other way) before they could get back to the New Terrace, we would be gone.

Yes, it is stupid, but we saw it as a small victory.

New Terrace

I had some friends growing up there that I've lost touch with, like Ronnie. He was a small guy but a good kid, and a buddy. One day we found a big wooden spool (about four feet across) like they use for power line wires. I got a few slats out of the middle part and talked Ronnie into getting in.

Before he knew what was happening, I was rolling him down the sidewalk as fast as I could, and he was screaming to high heaven. His mom was home, and she came running out in slippers and a housecoat (I think she was getting ready for work) yelling at me "Stop that at once!"

I grabbed the big wheels and stopped the spool. Got my hands full of splinters but got the spool stopped and got Ronnie out. Ronnie's mom came over to us and I thought she was going to smack me- or at least chew me out, but she didn't- just gave me a dirty look, grabbed her dizzy son, and took him home. I spent the rest of the day trying to get the splinters out of my hands. … If you try this at home, wear gloves.

On that same sidewalk a few months later, I brought my mom out for the maiden flight of my new rocket car. I built a standard type rocket body, though I attached a second tube on top and connected it so the parachute could come out from the back like a drag car. I put struts and big model airplane tires all around, stretched a string all the way down the sidewalk, and slid the rocket onto it.

It would have worked. But, in my haste, I had the fuse a little too close to the string…. So when I lit it, as it burned down… the string broke. Milliseconds later the rocket launched and with no string to guide it down the sidewalk, it headed right for my mom on the front porch.

Just missed her, hit the wall behind her, and made a big burn on the paint. Not much was left of the rocket car and I don't think my mom would ever watch me launch another rocket- of any type.

Across that same sidewalk a few months later, a kid got shot and killed. He wasn't even from the terrace... but was trying to get a baseball game up and going with the local kids. While he was in the kid's living room, two of them started fighting over a cigarette.

Just then, their little brother grabbed a .22 caliber rifle from their attic and shot the kid that was trying to break-up the fight. He shouldn't have been there; wasn't even from here. But now he was gone. The kid that was trying to get up to a baseball game... he didn't even belong there, but he was dead. I guess it was judged an accident, then ... a few years later when the shooter came back from the groovy-juvie, he was bragging about taking the boy's life.

For all the problems, growing up in the Terrace was probably just like growing up anywhere else in the '60's. We rode bikes everywhere (no helmets), went to the Boy's Club, and spent many summer afternoons wrestling in the side yard, or walking to the mall - always barefoot.

The first few trips to the mall (Colonial Plaza) were always tough. We had to wear shoes in school, so everybody was a tenderfoot, though as soon as school was out for summer, the shoes were off. Walking to the Colonial Mall required walking across the huge parking lot, and that was tough the first few times; that asphalt was hot. We would run from light pole to light pole (there was a concrete base around the light poles, much cooler than the asphalt) or the occasional rain puddle (it rains almost every afternoon during the summer). It took a while, but within a few weeks we could walk it- slowly- with no breaks.

Today you can't go into the mall without shoes, so I guess everybody in central Florida today is a year round tenderfoot.

Colonial Plaza 1960

I hung out mostly with normal kids. Slot cars, wrestling, playing a game on the swing sets where the goal was to kick the other swingers out of their swing. We did our best to have fun, always trying to get the girls to play doctor (old habits are hard to break). Yeah- just average kid stuff.

I avoided most of the thugs. There were a bunch of them. They were doing drugs, stealing shit, fighting, and actually having sex. Most soon got sent to the groovy-juvie or jail. Many died. Some in the Army, some shot by other thugs, some shot by cops, and some from drugs. One of my brothers, Clark (two years younger), got in with those thugs. As a result he's spent his entire life in and out of prison. Such a waste.

One night after I had given a bunch of the thugs a ride-probably so they could buy some dope- I was at the playground and heard a crack coming from my car. I ran up to find my new 8-track player had been stolen. I went after the guys and got my 8-track back. They threatened me and beat my ass, but I got my 8-track player back. I learned a lesson that night: those tough kids weren't so tough if you called them out, and that night I had called them out. They were just a bunch of scared kids, too.

I left the Terrace soon after; I was young by most standards, but not by ours.

Chapter Three

You do belong somewhere, just not here

I went to the elementary school mostly in Winter Park, and walked home to my grandma's house every day. I spent second grade in Altamonte Springs but that was short lived, and I was soon back to Killarney Elementary. I was even the host for Kinder Time (a local PBS Program) when our school put on a play. Killarney Elementary was a good grade school. I think I only got spanked once- and deserved it. I was throwing rock hard lima beans at some girl I probably had a crush on and as luck would have it, she ducked- and I hit the tattletale red haired girl sitting behind her.

After Killarney Elementary I went to Howard Jr. High School. I was working almost every day after school for a Lebanese guy who owned a gas station on my way home. While making a little money (pumping gas, checking oil, cleaning windshields) the owner let me do some simple mechanical work and I learned a bunch about fixing cars. He was a good boss but I had no idea where Lebanon was at that time. I found out later, of course.

I had a crush on a girl that sat next to me in Math Class. Nina was her name, and man... even her name sent warm waves through me. I went to confess my love several chapters into the math text, but by the time I had got there to do it, things had changed; she was 'otherwise involved', and I had to erase my love letter quickly before she saw it. So much for romance in Junior High School.

Then there was Boone High School. This was during the time of 'bussing'; they were bringing in black students from the other side of town.

Orlando was literally divided by railroad tracks; one side was white and one side was black. Most of the high school staff really seemed to hate the black students coming in from the wrong side of the tracks and made no effort to welcome them. But all things considered I think they hated the poor white kids a little more.

This was my first real experience with lots of rich white people. Allow me to be specific about who I considered rich at the time. If you had a dad, went out to eat (ever), picked up KFC on the way home or had a car that wasn't falling apart, you were rich. If you could miss a day of work, lived in your own home, or could go on vacation (ever), you were really rich. Man, you were skunk rich. All the kids at Boone High were skunk rich. It seemed like they really did not want us invading their preparatory school, too. Not just the kids, but the teachers and guidance counselors too. Guidance counselors now that is a great title. My guidance counselor told me (after spending two minutes in my file) that I should maybe try to get into Diesel Mechanics and got me transferred to a local vocational school. It was a happy day for Boone High and me, one more poor white boy out of their program.

To be fair I didn't put lots of work into High School. I was working nights and making good money. That's what mattered at the time. I was just waiting on my 16th birthday so I could drop out.

I later got a Florida High School Equivalency and earned degrees in Philosophy, Physics (Summa Cum Laude) and a MS in Electrical Engineering. Maybe that Guidance Counselor should have spent an extra minute in my file.

Chapter Four

Boy's Got To Work

My grandfather- the only male in my life during my childhood- and, as I may have mentioned, a bit of a hard ass. He made me turn over his entire garden at least once a year. It seemed like miles, but was probably about an acre. He also made me chop and split all his firewood. I remember splitting a huge pile of logs- he held the chisel, and I swung the sledgehammer. I was scared I'd miss and hit him, instead. His response to that? "Don't miss". I didn't.

We split a bunch of wood that day. I learned a lot about hard work from my Grandpa. He raised lots of animals, including rabbits. My younger brother by seven years, Kirk, was in charge of feeding them after school. In the spring we would butcher the rabbits, but never when Kirk was home.

On one occasion, just after finishing up about 20-25 rabbits, my brother came home from school and saw all the cages open.

"What happened!" he'd cried.

My grandpa replied, "Well you must have left the cages open. That dog next door must have got those rabbits."

That sounded better than telling the kid we would eat them on Sunday for months- what we would instead call a four legged chicken. Twenty years later I later told my brother the truth about the great rabbit loss, and he told me he hated and tormented the dog next door. Every time he saw it he would throw rocks and sticks! That poor dog had to endure all that treatment and never even got to eat one rabbit.

Remember when I said I was just waiting until I could drop out of school to start working? That started early. I did what I could to help my mom and started working at about 10. Now, the jobs you can get at that age are... interesting. I sold Grit newspapers door to door, got an old lawn mower and started mowing lawns- and even worked on a worm farm. If you ever wondered how they get fishing worms in those cardboard containers that they sell at the bait shop, allow me to enlighten you. I don't know how they do it today, but in the late 60's you'd start with a bunch of raised beds full of dirt and worms. Then you throw in kids that can count to 50 and know to only count the big worms, and, well- you can figure it out from there. I guess they'd have to use kids, because who else can spend all day bent over on their knees?

I also picked lots of oranges and tangerines. Picking oranges was alright, but I never liked picking tangerines. Never liked eating them much after that either. And rich farmers? Well. They're lumped in with the tangerines.

In Junior High School, so about 13 or 14, I got a job at a gas station working for a Lebanese guy who started teaching me about car engines. The guy was cool and always had advice on what we should do with our girlfriends... as if any of us had girlfriends. I pumped gas, washed windows, checked the oil and belts. When we were slow, I got to work on some of the cars. It was a cool after school job for a junior high kid.

I got a job at a factory where my mom worked drilling holes in Clackers. Clackers are plastic resin balls connected by a string. You pour plastic resin into glass molds and at first we inserted the string right in them. The strings would pull out, so we started drilling the plastic balls and feeding a string through (with a knot on the end). I think my uncle invented them and we made and sold a lot of them. They were fun to play but dangerous. They are like a fidget-spinner combined with a bolo (South American weapon). OK, a bit more dangerous than a fidget-spinner, you hold the string in the middle and clack the balls together. My mom (and a bunch of other women) mixed and poured colorful epoxy resin into the 2" diameter glass molds. I would drill a hole through two of them and another worker would feed and knot a string through and then a third would package the clackers for sale.

An old photo of clackers

I am pretty sure there were lots of kids with bruised and broken arms, a few choking deaths and a couple of nasty lawsuits by the time Clackers were taken off the market.

I also worked in a factory (with my mom) making sunglasses with earrings attached called The Eyes Have It. I ran 'The Sonic Sealer' for a few weeks. I'm not sure how long these glasses/earrings were on the market or in production but I got replaced by the owner's son. My first hard lesson in politics, but It would not be my last.

At 15 I had been around a bit and got a job at the OSO tri-county bus maintenance facility at night (and still going to school during the day). I changed oil, greased, and swept the buses (mostly the latter). I worked nights and got off at 5am, man I needed a car.

For my 16th birthday I was legally allowed by the state of Florida to drop out of school and allowed by my mom to smoke in the house. Probably does not sound like much of a present to you but for me it was the best present anybody could ever get for their birthday.

I soon went to Chattanooga TN, with my buddy Charles and worked drywall, if you have never done it, it is hard damn work. I also got another Ford Falcon but this one was a convertible; I loved that car and will get another one someday. Met a girl, we kissed a lot. I think she was promised to some guy in the Navy and we never went any farther than kissing in the front seat but man we kissed a lot.

When I returned to Orlando I was ready for full time employment and went to work for Belk Lindsey (department store) as a stock boy. Within a year they built a new store and combined the warehouse in the same building. I became a Loading Dock Forman. I had a crush on the beautiful girl that worked in cosmetics. One night she had a party and invited everyone at Belks including me. I drank too much and probably passed out. The next morning I woke up in the bed of our host, the beautiful young woman who worked in cosmetics. I don't know if anything happened but she kissed me on the cheek as I was leaving and then would not ever talk about it again. She got married soon after and I am sure has a wonderful life. The moral is, don't drink too much, you might miss something really special.

Belk's was great until I found out I made exactly the same as a lazy pot-head that worked up stairs. I had to sign for every piece of freight in and out and he had no responsibility at all. He also showed up stoned (most days) and left his pay stub on my desk. I moved on.

Ice Cold Auto Air

Next I was working for Ice Cold Auto Air fixing auto air conditioning. Mostly just changing parts but I learned how to diagnose and fix AC systems. It was a good job and I met some guys I'll never forget. One guy, Les, was the manager and he could play pool like nobody I'd ever met. He was a pool shark, maybe not the best pool shot I ever met but damn close.

We would hang out at a bar called the Clock after work most days. I was underage but was a big dude, never caused any trouble and was also a damn good pool shot (thanks to the Boy's Club).

One night I was sitting at the bar talking to the bartender (Satan, I can't make this up). I had a little hero worship going because he has a 1950's truck with a fiberglass breast attached to the glove box. Coolest thing I had ever seen.

Anyway all my buddies from work were sitting in the corner telling jokes and up to no good and when I returned from a bathroom trip I found an Army Recruiter sitting next to my beer at the bar. My buddy Les was grinning like a possum, I was set up. I sit down and this guy knew what was up. He said "I think your buddies set you up but as long as I'm here…"

Chapter Five

Boys Got to Have a Car

———— 1966 Ford Falcon Four Door Sedan ————

My best buddy Johnny had a girlfriend named Venus in the neighborhood (great girl, I hope they stayed together) and his girlfriend's dad had a 1960 Ford Falcon parked in front of his house that didn't run- I bought the car for $25.

My other buddy Charles had another Falcon about the same year that had a blown engine and we pulled it over to my parking lot. I swapped parts between those cars until I got the first one to run.

I was mobile baby. No license and probably no legal license plate (and surely no insurance) but I figured out a way to make it work. I even installed an 8-track tape player (playing Led Zeppelin). I was mobile, keep me moving.

———— Pushbutton Chrysler ————

About the same time I bought a 1956 Triumph, rebuilt the motor and basically used it as a trail/off road bike. My brother Clark was always stealing it while I was at work. One morning I switched the plug wires.

That afternoon when he tried to start it he got thrown over the handlebars. There was a lot of compression on those old bikes, no compression release and kick start only.

My brother hurt his leg, my mother was mad, Clark never stole my bike again.

After the '60 Falcon I had another. '64 I think convertible 2 door (I'm going to get another someday). I really wanted a Fairlane but they were expensive (I have both a convertible and Hardtop 66 Fairlane GT's today). After that came a long and not impressive list of Junkers but I did have a Buick with a Divan (a flat couch with a couple of pillows in back), that car was kind of cool.

Sylvia had a Datsun B210 when we got married and we drove that the entire time we were in the Army. I later got an Audi 100 LS (very cool car) and then my current favorite.

My current favorite is a 1959 Chevy ½ ton, step side, small window pickup. I still have it. It has gone through many transformations but mostly been a 327 powered, 4 speed (muncie) transmission and posi track rear end. I bought this truck almost 40 years ago from a cop that lived down the street from my father-in-law. I picked up the cab and frame at first and went back for the bed the next day.

It seems the kids had been using the bed as their sandbox and were not happy to see me take it. Both my kids learned to drive in the truck (Volare front clip, power steering, power brakes). Today it has been transformed into a pro-street truck with a narrowed 9-inch rear and really fat tires.

In addition I have 2 1950" Chevy pickups, a '41 Studebaker Coupe Hotrod and a cherry 1963 Chevy II SS all awaiting restoration next to my shop.

On my lot I also have a bunch of picture cars and personal cars I used making movies (more on that coming soon), but here's a few- just to help you imagine.

- *1966 Ford Fairlane 2 Dr Hardtop GT (mine, no movies)*
- *1966 Ford Fairlane 2 Dr Convertible GT, big block (mine, no movies)*
- *1971 Chevy Camaro Z28 (Mine, no movies)*
- *1967 GMC Handi-Van (Good Night Sleep Tight, Killers Van and The Locksmith mobile locksmith van)*
- *1974 Ford F250 dually Flatbed (Process Truck)*
- *1975 K10 4wd Chevy Pickup (Radio Silence-Federally Vehicle and The Dead of Night- Bad Guys Truck)*
- *1976 K10 4wd Chevy Pickup (The Dead of Night- Heroine's Truck)*
- *1978 Plymouth Volare 4 dr (Hero Car-Wander)*
- *1988 Ford Mustang Convertible (bought for commercial but no movies)*
- *1991 Ford F150 PU (Hero truck-The Locksmith)*
- *1994 Chevy C10 long bed PU (locations truck)*
- *1996 RV (hair/makeup)*
- *1996 Trailer (wardrobe)*
- *1996 Mercedes SL550 Coupe Convertible (mine, no movies)*
- *2003 Ford F250 4 dr (locations/personal)*
- *2008 Ford F550 4 dr. dually Flatbed (process truck)*
- *2015 Cadillac Escalade (pickup/deliver actors from airport)*

I also had two box trucks and a bus, but they got sold. That's another story for later on- worth telling! So why does *anybody* need over 20 cars? Well in truth they don't and honestly if you don't drive them and maintain them they quickly deteriorate.

But you know I just love old cars and I'll bet by the time this is finished I have one or two more (and maybe sell a couple).

Chapter Six

The Army's the best thing that ever happened to me

So I'm sitting in this bar, and my buddies just set me up with an Army Recruiter- remember, his office was across the street. My friends had thought it was funny the whole recruitment thing- but they have no idea how much they helped me that day.

He started talking about training and going to college, nobody from the Terrace ever went to college. So, I listened. A few days later I'm across the street, in the recruiter's office, taking the test. He got the results, smiled, and sat me down.

"OK first, you're smart". No, that's not true; they told me in high school I'm a stupid kid. "Yes, you're real damn smart and you *are* going to work on missiles, computers and radars."

"No. No, at best *maybe* I could work on trucks. This is a mistake." This guy was on something, I'd been sure of it.

"Sorry son. The Army does not make mistakes; you are going to a yearlong school to learn how to test and fix missiles, launchers and OMTS in the Hawk missile system 24D20, the test is never wrong. And after that you're going to college on the GI Bill." I'm sure he was wrong, but I signed up anyway.

Basic at Ft. Knox, KY was a surprise. First, we got there early and were stuck in a holding area for a few days. Man,

I heard this was tough, but this is a cakewalk. Everybody is nice, they gave us uniforms, filled out a bunch of forms, got haircuts, shots, got to go to the mess hall and eat, the PX sometimes to get razor blades and even a soda if we wanted it. Everything I had heard about basic training was bull, this was going to be easy.

Then early one morning, it happened, we met the real Drill Sergeants and I to this day believe my Senior Drill Sergeant is the meanest man that ever lived. He was fresh back from multiple tours in Vietnam, always pissed off and generally hungover.

Being from Florida I didn't have lots of experience with snow but I learned during my winter at Ft. Knox. Florida is also pretty flat but Ft. Knox has three training areas called Misery, Agony and HeartBreak. Maybe they are not the biggest peaks in the world but after you march up one you will think they are.

Basic was tough but I kind of liked it. I was certified as Expert with an M-16 and hand grenade, got a National Defense Service Ribbon (Vietnam was still going) and was promoted to PFC before I left. Next stop Ft. Bliss, Texas.

When I arrived at Ft. Bliss in 1974, I didn't have a nickel in my pocket but we got set up and moved into the barracks. Classes were cool: Basic Electricity, Basic Digital and all kinds of stuff I didn't know about but wanted to know. We also lost lots of people during those first few weeks. A couple of guys got caught smoking pot, gone. Some guys failed tests, also gone.

———— U.S. Army National Defense Ribbon ————

In all we lost over half the army people who started but were soon joined by a bunch of Marines (just before we started the real system training). I liked the Marines; they were disciplined but crazy. The recruiter was right, I was smart and at the top of my class. Who knew?

My best buddy and bunkmate, Clint, was going out with a girl from Las Cruces, New Mexico (about 45 miles away). Another guy was supposed to meet some other new girl from Cruces but Clint didn't like the guy so he brought me instead. We went to some house in downtown El Paso, and when we walked into their living room, there sat the most beautiful girl I ever saw.

Sylvia was stunning and way out of my league. We said hi but were both shy I guess so I spent most of the next hour talking to Chickie, Sylvia's cousin. Chickie is blind but was really cool and outgoing. As we were getting ready to leave and Chickie asks me "Well are you going to ask her out or what?" I was a little surprised then she said "You have been staring at Sylvia this whole time, now are you going to ask her out or not?"

I did, she said yes, in three months we were married, 49 years later we are still married. Sure glad I went that day.

Vietnam officially closed on April 30, 1975. If you ever meet anyone younger than me they didn't serve in Vietnam (unless they were Vietnamese).

We were all in school at Ft. Bliss at that time but don't remember many Soldiers were being sent over after late 1974. I graduated (about 40 people started the class 11 finished) and ended up second (to Clint). He got promoted to SP4 and got orders for Germany, I remained a PFC and got orders for Key West. A Hawk Straff Battalion (four batteries) got placed in Key West by President Kennedy during the Cuban Missile Crisis in 1962.

Twelve years later they were still there. Key West is over 200 miles from Miami but only 90 miles from Havana. Low flying planes could get under conventional Radar systems and surprise the mainland, but they could not fly under Hawk radars on 100' towers.

Radar added to tower in Key West

Hawk Missile Battery, Key West

Sylvia agreed to marry me (I don't know why!). We both wanted to get married in the church. The problem was that the Army would not pay for the move to Key West and as a PFC I only made $75 a month so I devised a plan.

The day I was scheduled to leave we went to the El Paso Courthouse and got married with a honeymoon that consisted of her taking me to the airport. But we got paid for housing and separate rations (almost doubled my take home pay) and with that extra money we were able to get married in the church three months later and move to Key West. Well, it was almost Key West. We lived in a tiny trailer on Stock Island on Pequena Lane. We were together but broke. If not for care packages sent by her sisters and leftover hot dogs and hamburgers from battery parties, I don't think we would have made it.

Then Jake-the-Snake (he had been a Marine in Vietnam, now an Army Staff Sergeant) found us a place in Key West, it was perfect, it was beautiful. Jake and his wife Doris got the landlord to let them empty out and fix up an apartment on the back of the house they were living in. It was great, floor to ceiling windows, fruit trees in the back yard really a beautiful place. He also got me a part time job at the bowling alley on the Navy Base fixing pinsetters. At about the same time Sylvia got a job at Sears (customer service) and I got promoted about that time to E4, Live was good.

At the same time I had to go see the battery education officer. Nice guy. He set me up with the Florida High School Equivalency, he said I had to go take it and I did. The Army would not promote me if I didn't have a high school diploma, so I got one.

A week later I got called back to the education office and there was a stack of books on the desk. He says they were mine, take them, he had signed me up for come college courses.

"What? I don't have time. I have duty and a part time job."

"Well," He said, "I already bought them and if you don't sign up I'll have to pay for them."

So I took them.

Every semester the same thing would happen, he would sign me up and I had to take the course. This guy changed my life, would not let me quit, would not let me slack off. I graduated just before I got out of the Army with an Associate degree from St. Leo's College. Nobody I ever knew had a college degree.

I finally made E-5 about the time we came back to Fort Bliss in El Paso to fire a missile (called Annual Service Practice).

Usually when ASP was over and you had a good score (like we did) the entire battery went to party in Juarez, Mexico. I had brought Sylvia with and went to join her in Las Cruces for a couple of days but what happened in Mexico to the guys is a good story.

Apparently one of the senior guys, highly intoxicated, went to a room with some pretty young thing and not long after came back very happy. So happy we wanted his number two guy to experience that same experience with the young girl and he paid for it. The second guy reluctantly went up-stairs as well then after getting hands-on during the experience discovered the young woman had some extra equipment. While this was going on the senior guy was gushing about it being the finest sexual experience he had ever known. About that time the second comes running down the stairs yelling that it was a dude, sure that his senior had set the whole thing up as a joke.

C 1/65 ADA Crew

I heard about this and may have harassed the fellow a bit, just a little bit. Years later as a civilian I was working out of Ft. Bliss and out of the building I'm going into comes this same guy. We both stopped shaking hands and I may have smiled a bit. He dropped my hand and lost his mind. "F*** you Scoughton, I didn't know it was a dude." he left, and I have not seen him again. I never said a word, just smiled.

The next year was hard work and good friends. Jake and Doris were like family. Sylvia and I had our first kid in

Key West, Troy Jr. He was the hairiest kid in the hospital and I was sure it had to do with my manliness. All the hair soon fell off and he looked just like any other beautiful baby boy. Jake and Doris got transferred to Germany. Sylvia, Troy Jr. (then three months old) and I reenlisted and came back to Ft. Bliss for another school.

We came back to Ft. Bliss so I could learn to become a 24G (different Radar, same system). Sylvia got pregnant again on the way over (I suspect in Winter Park at my grandparents' house in the Blue Room). There is an old wives' tale about not being able to get pregnant while you are breast-feeding. I am here to tell you that is a lie.

I went back to school at Ft. Bliss. We had a small class with about half Marines. They would not march for anybody but me (I called cadence, the other Army E5 in the class was a bit wimpy). Damn I loved those guys. After graduation my beautiful daughter Tiffany was born and 30 days later, I was on my way to South Korea.

B 2/71 was a couple clicks from the DMZ on top of a mountain. Our base camp was Camp Irwin in Pob Won Ri and called the Cugie Compound by the locals. Some claimed it had been a MASH compound. Who knows? But I'll bet every little outlying compound on the DMZ claims to be the MASH compound. South Korea of 1977 is way different from the South Korea of today but I endeared myself from day one like always.

——————— Work at B 2/71 ———————

My first week my unit was in the field and I was busting ass getting the system set up, your life could depend on how quickly you can emplace and get it operational. In Key West (highly trained STRAFF units) everybody from the battery commander on down was humping cables pounding ground stakes pulling generators into place when we went to the field. We had a 15-minute emplacement time (AFU) and sought to meet (or beat) that emplacement time every time we moved. These guys in Korea were right on the DMZ and should have been on top of their game but they were slow.

Half hour into our emplacement I'm chewing out some private for moving like a snail and he points to the ridge and asks about those guys. I look up and see every other section chief (other than myself), the battery commander, both LT's and platoon sergeants all outlined on a ridge overlooking the emplacement festivities. I ran up the ridge ready to fight and grabbed the first guy I came to (that was my rank). I endeared myself

"First off asshat, you never outline yourself like this, and secondly don't expect your guys to do what you won't do yourself." I chewed all their asses, told them "If you won't help, then at least hide." and went back down the hill and back to work.

It took forever (probably an hour) but we finally got the system up. The guys I was working with had a little more spring in their step after my demonstration. Senior staff didn't like me much after that, but most were short and RAMF's (rear area M.F.) anyway. Our next field problem was a little better (maybe 45 Minutes). We never got to be as good as a STRAFF Battery, but we got better over the year I was there and even passed our yearly Missile Fire exercise.

_____ B 2/71 and C 2/71 Admin Area Camp Irwin _____

We had problems with drugs (mostly codeine) and the black market. Our guys would get mixed up in stupid shit and get in big trouble. Beta tape machines had just come out and were all the rage. I never really got the whole story but understand some enterprising Airmen (soldiers are not near enterprising enough) had secured a beta machine, some lights and a camera (or two) and were shooting porn with some of the local prostitutes and soldiers (it had to be Soldiers because most Airmen are not properly equipped). I'm sure porn was illegal in Korea at the time but I guess that did not stop the desire to have a copy and a machine to watch it on.

The black market deal was you would get the money to buy the Beta machine from the PX in Seoul and a mail receipt showing you shipped it home. Everybody is happy right. There was just one catch; the factory box was too big to mail through the post office. So the MP's would call you in and ask you what happened to the Beta player you bought. You told them you mailed it home of course and here is the mail receipt. "OK, how did you do that?"

The GI would answer, "I took it to the Post Office and sent it home." "In the factory box?" They asked if you answered "yes". Then, MP's told you, "You are under arrest. The factory box is too big to mail home through the post office. You would have to put the unit in a smaller box".

I knew a guy that was a damn fine NCO who went from SSG (about to make E7) to E4 to PV2 to civilian within a few months. I met him at a gas station out off I-10 in the middle of nowhere. We were driving back to Orlando on leave and he told me the whole story. He is a truck driver now and I hope living a great life.

We also got women stationed with us for the first time. That had never happened before. Women were never stationed with front line combat units but in 1977 in South Korea that changed and we got several women transferred into our unit. I remember one Como Sergeant who came in at that time. I really didn't know her well but broke up a fight between two hard heads who had both decided that she was going to be their girlfriend. After I separated the guys and put them to doing some miserable task as punishment I went to see the female Como Sergeant. I was angry. I mean I don't care who she dated but lets not have my guys killing each other over her. She was a big girl, tough and I think it was good I kept my tone in check but I was pissed. It turns out she didn't know either of the guys.

I only stayed in the service for another year or so but I know that integration of women into all aspects of the military was filled with incidents just like this. I'm sure by now it is no longer a problem but I am equally sure that there will always be problems that must be dealt with swiftly (scrubbing the bathroom with a toothbrush works pretty good).

My last year I returned to Ft. Bliss and got inserted into a group making training videos, at building 500 on Ft. Bliss. I got to make a training video on radar synchro-alignment that I thought was really good. I was awarded two ARCOMS (one was an MSM but got downgraded), and a good conduct medal. I finally made E6 (but had to reenlist to pin it on). In my last month I got several sets of orders almost on the same day and my warrant officer application returned (denied).

On our dinner table Sylvia and I were looking at several sets of orders to return to Korea, orders for Elapsed Time in Service (ETS), orders for E-6 (SSG), reenlistment orders and of course my denied Warrant Officer application. My reenlistment date was close.

SSG was something I really wanted but I was going back to Korea again, another year away from my family. If I would have made Warrant Officer, I might have stayed in but we went through all the sets of orders and accepted the ETS orders.

It was time to get out of the Army and go to college full time.

U.S. Army Housing at Biggs Field

Chapter Seven

New Mexico, State University

My wife Sylvia was born and raised in Las Cruces, New Mexico, a great little town and home of NMSU. While I was in Korea one of the other section chiefs had a daughter that was going to school at NMSU in engineering and he told me that NMSU was highly rated in Electrical Engineering.

_______ *NMSU Thomas Brown (EE Department)* _______

I knew how to fix radars but I didn't really know how they worked. I mean I got the basics in the Army but I wanted to know everything about the process, I wanted to design them. I went to NMSU to meet with Dr. George Lucky and signed up for the EE program. I was worried I would never make it.

Before I left the army most of the senior Sergeants told me I would come crawling back, that I would be broke and not able to make it away from the Army. The fact is that with the GI Bill, working at the VA Office and tutoring math at the Dona Ana Branch (a community college that is part of NMSU).

I made more money than I did in the Army. I got started, it was hard, it was different and it wasn't the Army. There were some smart kids who grew up in Los Alamos and were in calculus clubs in high school (really smart kids) but I worked hard and hung in there. I was good at it. I went to work for a guy named Dr. Sharp soon after I started at the VA office.

When we first met he was in a wheelchair and had no use of his legs and limited use of his hands. I was concerned but within 15 minutes I never considered him disabled again. He was sharp (no pun intended) and capable of doing whatever he wanted.

Fortunately for me and for the people of New Mexico, we were there to help people find their niche in life (and damn good at it). I help administer tests and also tutored folks who wanted to earn their high school equivalency with the GED test.

After all was said and done I earned four degrees:

- *AA in Philosophy from St. Leo's in Florida (Military Extension Program)*
- *AS/BS in Physics from Park College (Summa Cum Laude, Military Extension Program)*
- *MS in Electrical Engineering and Electromagnetics from New Mexico State University*

I thought about a PhD in EE but started racing dirt cars instead. As crazy as it sounds I think the education I got building Dirt Race Cars helped me develop the company I was soon to open, but I am getting ahead of myself again.

So an NMSU Aggie went to Harvard for a week and got lost on campus. "Hey man, where is the library at?" the cowboy asks a passing student.

"At Harvard, we do not dangle prepositions." the student replies.

"OK, so where is the library at, asshole?"

Chapter Eight

Boy's Got' To Have a Career!

After about a year at NMSU working as a student and instructor, a guy I knew (Eric, also an Army Veteran) told me that Raytheon was looking for technicians who had Hawk experience to work on fielding a new anti-aircraft system called Patriot.

I went for an interview in El Paso and got a job working for Raytheon Service Company teaching Patriot. My starting salary was 20K a year. That was really good money in 1981.

For school, I cleared it with my advisor, Dr. Lucky and was allowed to take classes at a military extension program through Park College (now Park University) that were offered at night and on the weekends at Ft. Bliss.

I started training soldiers but soon moved into Contractor Logistic Support (CLS) and training the senior guys. Patriot was an Air Defense Missile System like Hawk but on steroids. The Radar was a phase array steering the beam without physically moving the radar antenna, all done by applying a magnetic field to each antenna element as required to steer the beam. I know you probably don't care how this works but I could go on for hours, it is a grand design and the boys from Spencer Labs and Raytheon Company in Boston really outdid themselves.

So I have got to tell you one story. I went to Boston to teach some classes and was touring the manufacturing facility. I approached one system that had a hard failure (antenna control problems). At that time there were over 5000 elements and each was wired to maybe 8 to 10 wire wrapped pins.

I worked on computers with similar wiring while in the service and was damn good at finding problems. I went and got a Time Domain Reflectometer (TDR) from across the floor and started troubleshooting. Within about half an hour I had found the problem and fixed the faulty wire wrap, the system worked and I was a hero.

———— Patriot Missile System Launcher ————

Well not really. The Andover assembly building was a union shop. I was an engineer. So I lugged a piece of test equipment across the floor (fine). Fixed a radar that Technicians were supposed to fix (another fine) and then tested the system when rewired the faulty antenna element (you guessed it a fine) and then tested the system to make sure it was fixed (fine).

So instead of being happy my boss was livid because I cost his department about 40 hours in fines by fixing the radar that nobody could fix. Ever wonder why military systems cost so much and take so long to build?

I drove back and forth from Las Cruces to El Paso (about 45 miles) for a while, but I finally convinced Sylvia to move there while I was working in El Paso. We lived in El Paso but spent every weekend at her parent's house in Las Cruces. Eventually Patriot got fielded and I moved to a project at White Sands Missile Range (WSMR) writing code and running RF tests for the SEMIVAF. We moved back to Las Cruces. El Paso was good, but Las Cruces was home.

I graduated from Park College with a BS and AS in Physics (Summa Cum Laude) and now that I was working back in New Mexico, I started in a graduate program at NMSU (MSEE in Electromagnetics). A year passed driving to a multi-story windowless building in the middle of White Sands Missile Range (WSMR). Building 23628 housed one of the largest anechoic chambers in the world and was home of the Special Electromagnetic Interference Vulnerability Assessment Facility (SEMIVAF).

I got to work on some great programs there and I got to more with my original advisor Dr. Lucky. He was a great professor and the best engineer in Special Electromagnetic Effects (his field). He gently pushed me to get a master's degree telling me that if you wanted to be a real physicist you needed a PhD, but you could be an Engineer with a Masters (he was right) and that is what I did.

Most of what we worked on was classified as was the case for the rest of my career, but I can tell you this truth:

any electromagnetic signal can be interfered with (jammed), any electromagnetic signal.

Secondly any transmitted electromagnetic signal can be detected and its direction determined (DF-ed), any transmitted signal. If you have multiple direction finding detectors you can pinpoint the location of the transmitter.

So any received signal can be jammed and if you transmit a signal I can find it. Yes, that includes the spread spectrum and the other BS you may try to prevent this from happening. Just because you tell your government customer it is impossible to detect/DF/Jam this signal, don't make it so.

About a year after driving back and forth to the world's largest chamber and I suspect in part due to Dr. Lucky, I got offered a job at the Physical Science Laboratory (PSL) on the NMSU campus (the university's research and development arm).

PSL was great. Not only did I get to work on some of the best projects available with some of the best people available but I got to work with the man who would later be my business partner and one of the best engineers in the business, Chris Ham.

_______ *Physical Science Laboratory NMSU (today)* _______

I was supposed to write Forth code but was almost immediately transferred to the Electromagnetics Group and went to work for a hard assed engineer named Al Waterman. Al did not take any crap from anybody but he loved and supported his engineers. We all went to lunch together almost every day and if anyone failed to make it, I believe it truly hurt Al's feelings. He also protected us from the administration. We were his guys and gals. I was able to walk across campus for classes and although traveling a lot (could be a hassle with classes) managed to make good grades and finish my Masters.

PSL had a world-class antenna range at the time and eventually I took over management of the range. The previous manager had given me a hard time when measuring one of my antenna projects but as soon as I took over he had a project that needed measurement. Payback is sweet, he had to follow all of the rules he made me follow.

One of the problems I encountered while running the range was with student employees. We had a bunch of them and many of them were brilliant. I even hired the first female student employee at the range. My supervisor (not Al, some new asshat) said no. He went on to say, "having some girl running up and down the towers in short-shorts would be a distraction to the young men working there".

I hired her anyway and got in trouble (my special talent). Don't get me wrong, she did look damn good running up and down those towers in short-shorts and I'm sure it may have been a distraction to some of the men working there but that was their problem, not hers. She was smart, hardworking and one of my best engineers on the site. She later went to work at Los Alamos and I'll bet she can still outperform any of those guys.

The problem with this whole story is that I could not offer her a job when she graduated. I had no slots and could not offer any of my students a job when they graduated, we just didn't have enough work and way too much overhead. It killed me to let them go and I would always remember the helpless feeling of watching them for another job leave after graduation.

HELP- We did some great projects at PSL and some were classified like a programmable EW system we build for BCPO the control system was programmed using Forth (a new code popular at the time and one I worked in). Very cool system but that is about all I can tell you about it.

MDHC Telemetry System- Chris Ham was project manager on the most capable Real Time Telemetry system ever made (and I helped). We built the system for McDonald Douglas Helicopter Company (in Mesa, AZ). They were performing flight-testing on the then new Apache Attack Helicopter. Before our system the Helo would go through a test scenario and record instruments on multitrack tape recorders on board. The next day they would then fly the tapes to their facility in California, then days later get the results and perform analysis. If the maneuver was missed they just had to re-fly it.

Our system used a real time data link from an RF system and antenna to a tracking ground system brought into one of the most capable computer systems ever made (at that time). We used 52, Motorola 68020 based cards in parallel, all running real time code that was in cache memory (no transfers) so written in assembly code smaller than 1K. Fritz Lawrence and Don Murphy (owners of Syndetix) wrote most of the code but I wrote the basic air data code. From the real time front ends the data flowed into two DEC 785 mainframes and then to a DEC 8550 main frame for display. I imagine Chris Ham and his group wrote most of that code and that was what interfaced the test engineers with the data coming from the helo under test.

At the time it was the most capable real time telemetry system on the planet. Chris got his Masters in EE based on this system and his Masters Tech Report. The customer could complete their analysis in real time and soon their California based aircraft company was sending their tapes to Mesa for analysis. I understand they paid for the system by charges to the other branch of their company just after delivery.

Chris, myself and several other engineers presented papers everywhere and as a result everyone copied our design.

Today you could probably have more computational power in a high-end workstation but at the time this one was the best. That was what PSL did, that was what we were known for.

DEC VAX Mainframe Computer

Next I designed and built a system to train Air Force precision approach radar operators how to work in an EW denied environment. The problem was that these radars were always being used to direct takeoff and landing of military aircraft. So I could not just go jam their systems in a conventional way, they were always in use and it was not possible. So I injected my bad guy signal into the system after the receiver, allowing us to jam parts of the system but leave the main system fully operational (and landing aircraft). I used a state of the art IBM desktop computer to control this system. It was a 486 based IBM machine, had a single 5-inch floppy drive, small hard drive and cost just over $10,000. I wrote a tech report on that one and that's how I got my masters. I can't and won't go into any more details on this system but can say it worked real well and trained lots of operators.

———— USAF Approach Radar Control Screen ————

I moved up in the organization and found myself Senior System Engineer, a position recently vacated by Chris Ham. Soon our section chief, Wade Craddock, moved on and his position became available. At his urging I applied for the job but I didn't get it. The woman who did was smart and had lots of experience in programming and project management. But soon we had problems.

I was working on a telemetry system for the High Speed Test Track at Holloman. We had another project come up with Georgia Tech Research Institute (GTRI) that was a bigger job and right in my wheelhouse. The design of this system for the High Speed Test Track was done and fabrication was in process, just needed to build it, test it then install it.

I had a new guy who I bought in and assigned him to this project to provide a cost-to-complete estimate. He finished his estimate then presented it to management while I was out of town. Not only did his estimate exceed funds remaining for the job but exceeded the original cost for the entire job.

When I returned and found out what happened I let my new section chief know that the estimate was way over and I was going to fire the guy from the project (maybe from the Lab), that he should have passed it by me first and that I should have been present for the presentation. What I didn't know at the time was that my new section chief and this bozo had a thing going (I only realized this later when I saw them together in a quiet restaurant holding hands and staring deeply into each other's eyes).

I was going to fire her new boyfriend. Politics is a harsh teacher; I went from Senior Systems Engineer and top on the list for Engineer of the Year to incompetent ass in under two days.

One of my old Section Chief's, Wade Craddock, was the only person in the organization who stood up for me at the time. Most of the management by then were retired Air Force Officers who had never designed or managed anything, but they could kiss ass with the best. I moved on that week, I am sad to say that PSL declined steadily over the next few years, and I have not worked with them again after that. I went to work for a little company that had a subcontract with PSL that I had been working with for several months.

Syndetix was a minority owned small business (8a) with contracts mostly with the Big Crow Program Office (BCPO). It was a couple of KC-135 aircraft modified with radomes that could be used to provide electronic warfare training. They also had several ground based systems for testing most military radar and electronic systems. I wish I could go into details, but the most I can say is that we did some really cool shit in a lot of exotic places. I ran the Electromagnetics Group, Chris Ham ran the Systems Group.

NKC-135 Big Crow Aircraft (3132)

If you want to make an effective Electronic Warfare system (you know, jam somebody) you need a computer system (control), radio (low power RF stuff), high power RF amp and a high power antenna (generally custom). The platform varies and could be: a fixed site, a lab, a vehicle, an aircraft (like Big Crow) or a high performance aircraft. Chris Ham could design control systems and write real-time machine code better and quicker than almost anybody (well, I'm pretty good at it too). I could design the custom antennas, transmission line and high power RF stuff.

Put us together and you have the complete EW system. Over the next seven years we built a bunch of cool stuff and built a ton of systems. We also won a bunch of contracts for Syndetix.

EMRE Test Facility - We won the contract to upgrade the Electro Magnetic Radiation Effects (EMRE) Test Facility at White Sands Missile Range, NM. The facility consisted of several ranges operating at different frequencies. The idea was to be able to test Military systems for vulnerabilities from high power radiation to insure high power EW weapons would not be effective.

One of our first test articles after completion of the system was an SUV. Apparently some of these SUV's had issues with deployment of their air bags when exposed to high power RF environments.

Imagine you are driving across the Golden Gate Bridge while an Aircraft Carrier is steaming out to sea. They turn on their Radar to test operation and your airbag deploys. Some might find that distracting. The antennas I designed for this system would handle more power (continuous) than any I knew of. It was a very cool system, operated for over 20 years and was later rebuilt a second time by TMC Design Corp.

Oil Spooge Processing System - When you pump oil out of the ground, it doesn't always look like the store-bought bottle for your car. The first few hundred gallons might be full of water, sand and other nasty stuff that is generally pumped into a ditch nearby. These quickly become large ponds of oil, water, dead animals and tumble weeds I call Spooge (it looks like tar). This is nasty stuff and the EPA really does not like it.

Some really smart guys at Carnegie Mellon Research Institute devised that you could subject this stuff to microwave energy to heat it up, then a centrifuge to remove the sediment and finally a coalseer system to remove the water. Another really smart guy who we had worked with was designing a filter for one of the systems on EMRE, George Harris (super smart and really nice guy) from Maine, got with some guys from Texas and built a system to test this theory on a large scale. I got tasked to make it work commercially.

Basically we made an antenna and tuner that could channel the match the large 1 Mhz microwave sources into a stream of spooge. The spooge would be pumped into the system but might change any second (amount of water, etc) so its impedance would change. The microwave transmitter wants to see the same impedance all the time at its wave guide. So I built a large high power tuner, rectangular to circular wave-guide and antenna (called an applicator) and

Chris built an auto tune control computer (Chris's real time code, Murphy's applications code) and we stuck it all in a van.

Basically we would pump in the spooge and blast it with microwave energy (heat it up) then send it to a centrifuge to spin out the sand/sediment and then to a coalescer to remove the water. This was a really cool and effective system and also unclassified.

It worked great as long as we ran it. As soon as we turned it over to the oil field operators they would break it. I think it needed more automation but I believe in the end it got sold to a Saudi Arabian company and moved there, maybe it is still working today.

What I remember most clearly from this project is the smell. As soon as you get into the area (Hobbs, NM) the smell of the oil is everywhere and gets into your hotel room, clothes, everything. You don't notice it after a few days but when I would return my wife would basically want me to change clothes in the garage and wash everything before I came into the house.

MONOTOA - This is a mono-pulse/time-of-arrival direction finding system that worked really well. That is all I'm going to say about this system but I will tell you a story about a field test we did in Nags Head, NC.

We had three systems set up around Chesapeake Bay and I was with the most southern system set up in a house that belonged to the wildlife preserve on the outer banks, really one of the most beautiful places on the planet.

Anyway we were testing and when done for the day (or night) we would retire to our hotel in Kill Devil Hills area, not far from where the Wright Brothers made their famous first flight.

One night the weather got really nasty and a ranger came by; told us to evaluate because a hurricane was coming. I told him we had supplies and were tough Army contractors, so we'd be OK. He told us that the only reason we got to use this house is because it was condemned and would probably fall down during the storm.

We packed and went to the hotel.

The Project Manager was angry for us having left our post in the middle of the test. Again, national television came to my defense, the CNN storm trackers were just outside our hotel with a live broadcast as the storm made landfall. The PM turned on the TV, saw the storm on CNN, apologized, then canceled the test.

The three guys that owned Syndetix always talked to their employees about dividing profits and giving bonuses to the employees that brought in the work and built the systems. I imagine all small companies talk that way while they are growing. Then one day, they make some money and everything changes. They decide to forget about those that earned the money and keep it for themselves. 'It *is* their company after all'. I frequently called them on it.

They didn't like that and decided to replace me.

A buddy of mine that worked for another RF company in Austin gave me a call one day and asked for my dregs. "What are you talking about man? I got none." He then went on to tell me that he had seen our ads for Emag guys and needed some good people himself. "Look, just keep the best ones- that's fine- just send me anybody you don't need. I need some people, man". I got him to send me the ad- it was for my position. It had been running for a month.

That day I went to see our primary customer at Kirtland AFB in Albuquerque. The night before I called Chris Ham. We had been talking about the big bonus (or lack of bonuses was more like it) and the fact that we wrote all the proposals, bid the work, and then managed it and built the systems after we won. All they had was the contract and a good credit line. We really did not need Syndetix. Yeah, all they had was the contract and a bunch of money… Years of experience, a building, employees, you know… small stuff like that. After a long and tense discussion, Chris and I decided I would approach our prime government customer, Milt, the next morning about forming a new company and ask if he might ever do business with us.

Milt was a complex dude. He had single handedly built the Big Crow Program Office (BCPO) from almost nothing. He now had two KC-135 aircraft and a multitude of ground EW systems, most built by Chris Ham and myself. He had customers from all services and could handle nearly any EW mission.

Mostly training at that point, but also looking at operational missions, the first was Bosnia 1. We had planned the mission for Bosnia 1 for months but it was later handled by a 500-pound bomb, it turns out that properly placed a 500-pound bomb can be very effective for any kind of system. After thrashing around for weeks in Albuquerque, I was up early at the hotel having breakfast and saw the system we were studying in flames on the morning news feed. I called the government counterpart and told him that I would be sleeping in that morning and see him later. He had a fit until I convinced him to turn on the morning news.

Bosnia 2 was a little more hands-on, a nearly six-month forward deployed that I ran part of (technical side). Worked with some great folks from the U.S. Army, got to see some cool countries. BCPO had now added combat support missions to their training missions. At this point the Army and Air Force had both done away with EW assets so this is what they had in the US arsenal. I had known and respected Milt for several years. At this point I knew Milt well and he knew me. I was always a by-the-rules guy (especially when deployed) and he was a little looser in that area but we liked and respected each other.

Back to that fateful morning when I asked about forming a new company, well I was still afraid Milt might tell me to pound sand and get out of his office but he surprised me. He told me that I was his antenna guy and that Chris was his systems guy and he didn't care who we worked for we were going to build his stuff. He would instruct Synedtix to cut us a subcontract. People can bad mouth Milt Boutte all they want, but he has done some great things for this country. He may not have always followed every rule, but he always had the best interest of his aircraft, his programs and his country in focus.

Troy Scoughton, Mike Bowden and Chris Ham (Troy, Mike & Chris or TMC) formed TMC Design Corporation the next day.

Chapter Nine

TMC Design Corporation

Everybody, including me before I did it, thinks running a company is easy. You just sit back and let everybody else do the work, collect a bunch of money and get rich, right. Well not exactly. Syndetix was forced by BCPO to give us a subcontract but they were not happy about it and set out to put us out of business as soon as possible. We struggled with everything including a name but finally agreed on TMC (Troy, Mike and Chris) Design only to find there was a graphics design company of the same name in town but they soon went out of business. We also did not know of the Texas Medical Center when we filed for our corporate papers but by then it was too late. We bought a computer and a good printer. We rented an office and bought a copy of Quick Books. We had one contract reluctantly given to us by our former employer. We were legit.

My lovely wife, Sylvia, was an RN working at the local hospital and it is a good thing because I did not get paid for the first year we were in business. Syndetix awarded us the sub-contract but they were stingy and questioned every charge. It was soon apparent that we needed our own contracts if we were going to make it and we needed an 8a certification (minority owned small business) in order to win those government contracts. 8a certified companies could be awarded small contracts ($3M) without competition. A government engineer we all knew (and liked) was retiring from government service (SEMIVAF) and he talked him into signing on with us and he got 51% ownership of the company. Leroy Gomez came on and took over as CEO. We soon got certified as an 8a company and started getting our own contracts. The company grew.

At one point we had rented offices in the middle of town. Then more offices and a shop in an industrial area and another shop in West Mesa. I spent about all of my time in my truck driving from one location to another. It was not working.

A few years after we opened we built a consolidated facility in Las Cruces and moved all of our facilities into one place. A few years later we purchased a second building in Colorado Springs and before we sold the business we had offices in Las Cruces, Colorado Springs, Huntsville, Orlando, Albuquerque, and Aberdeen (proposed).

_________ *TMC Design Corporation, Las Cruces* _________

I did not want to be just a services company (like most defense contractors). I wanted to build stuff. We started to acquire machine equipment and machinists. At first I built everything (I learned how to by building race cars, trailers and hotrods out of my garage). Eventually we built a world class welding shop, paint shop and sheet metal fabrication facility to go with the electronics fabrication and antenna design and test facility. We could manufacture anything. Whenever we could we would buy things off the shelf but often we could not find quality items and our customers needed the best.

One example was trailers. If you want to build a large (say 15 feet) mobile satellite communications antenna you need a good trailer. We could not find any, so I adapted a design I used for race cars and sent the design to our shop in Albuquerque. When I got up there I realized they had made it out of steel instead of aluminum (as I had asked), I thought it would be too heavy for air transport and the Army would hate it. It was tough, really tough, and the Army loved them and still use versions of these trailers. My guys made jigs and our mechanical engineers made exact drawings and we still make dozens of trainers today. They are heavy but will last forever.

We also hired lots of students for our COOP program. I had Electrical Engineering COOP working as technicians in our electronics shop. Mechanical Engineering COOP students worked in our machine shop. The idea was that the electrical guys would learn about circuit board and systems assembly (how to make cables and rack equipment) and the mechanical guys would learn how to read drawings, realistic tolerances and how the machines worked they would be sending their designs to in the future. They would also learn the language and form relationships with the technicians and machinists they would be working with in the future.

I would slowly ease them into design jobs as they grew and by the time they graduated (generally a couple of years but as much as four) they would be ready to become really good engineers that could design anything and communicate with and often help the people who built the stuff. I'm a hands- on guy and I like hands-on people.

Nearly all the students stayed to work for us after they graduated. They were trained, had a clearance and knew how we did business.

Our admin group was fed from the front desk. Same idea as with the COOP students, I hired every new admin person to first work the front desk then move them up as needed (and rehire the front desk position).

We built a world-class company that nobody knew, well nobody outside the government.

Chapter Ten

After 9-11 we deployed immediately. It took several weeks to get to the country and I learned some interesting facts along the way. Moròn Spain is not pronounced moron (like most Americans would pronounce it) and the locals will tell you about it immediately.

Egypt may be a cool place to visit but they don't like hordes of weird looking US civilians on undeclared business in their country. We were there under armed guard while my first grandchild was born.

We hit the ground, in an undisclosed location, got set up and after some weather delays (snow in the mountains) required for a coordinated attack, smoked them. To quote Tommy Franks " Boys we fucked them" that night. They had it coming and it felt good to deliver what they had ordered in New York City six weeks before.

After that first mission a few of us went home. I am a really good high power antenna designer and I had an antenna I needed to get out for another mission, I was done in three days. A week later (I am a pretty good antenna designer and builder) I was on my way back, this time on a C-17 with a bunch of Spec-Op guys.

I have flown on a bunch of transport planes. Our usual transport was a couple of modified KC-135's to be exact tail numbers 3132 and 8050. We used 8050 for missions over Afghanistan and never had a failure. The planes were maintained perfectly and performed. Our maintenance guys were the best.

Our pilots were a mixed bag, some great, some scared to death. They were all reading Harry Potter books at the time. Man, Air Force Officers, never catch a 10th Mountain commander (Army Commandos) reading Harry Potter.

I have also taken significant ground based equipment to various places (generally shitholes) on several transports including C-5A's but my favorite of all time aircraft is the C-17. I love them and buddy they can move some stuff. Just a great aircraft, if you got to go someplace shitty, this is the best way to get there.

Anybody that has ever been in a situation like this will probably tell you the same thing, three hours of unimaginable stress and performance at the highest level possible followed by several days (or weeks) of boring routine. Eat, workout, shower, go to sleep, wake up, make your cot, go to work, open your mouth, spout off, get your ass chewed out, repeat. In the end it was long hours, little sleep, knowing if you screwed up people you cared about could die, so lots of tension, mentally tough and mostly boring.

After returning the second time (a week later) I was in with a bunch of young Army Rangers and they just didn't know how to take me. Who is the old fat guy with a beard and long hair in the shower this morning? "Yea I saw him working out, he can push a little weight but needs to push himself away from the table". I was 45 and probably 275 lbs. (that is a lie). Most of these guys were 20 and a very fit 180 lbs., ran 6 miles every day, ate nails, posed for calendars.

Our best and our brightest. I sure hope all those guys made it back in one piece but know they didn't. I finally made my way back to our compound a few days later. We did some cool stuff but again I can't talk about it.

In my opinion we were done with our mission in 90 days. We kicked butt and I think we should have withdrawn at that point. Most of the Spec Ops guys went home after 90 days as did most of our guys. But we had a lingering mission (SAR), somebody had to stay, so I stayed. I was there for a couple more months and then relieved by, you guessed it, Chris Ham. I met some great people and got to know some people I already knew, better. Scott already worked for us but proved once again he was my right arm. Bruce (my brother from another mother) worked for another company but I convinced him to start his own company, he did and was wildly successful. If I could do it he could do it. Three of the soldiers with our outfit went to work for TMC after they retired. Then we got fired for following orders. Politics is a harsh teacher. More on that later.

I can only tell one cool story from that time. One morning I was just getting off, I worked 5pm to 5am every day. Unless something was going on it was always the same: I got on at 5pm, checked everything out, checked in with command, mostly drank coffee and waited for something to happen. I got off at 5am, went to breakfast, the gym and then crashed for a few hours, unless some ass hat needed me during the day, usually to chew me out for something I had no control over. So that morning I am walking around like a zombie about 8am going to our tent to crash and I see Mimi from the cast of the Drew Carry Show. I thought I was hallucinating but found out there was going to be a USO show later that day. Really? I got up early and caught the early show (at 2). They were great, funny and took everyone's mind off things for a while. I went to work at 5pm.

The next morning I was checking my perimeter just before I was to get relieved, about 04:45 and saw some moron (not from Spain) taking pictures. There must have been a dozen signs, in five languages, stating "No Photography Under Pain of Death", (or something like that) but this guy apparently could not read or didn't care. I alerted the guards, they tackled the guy and drug him and his camera over to me. It was Drew Carry and he was very happy to be recognized (the guards didn't know or care who he was).

Troy-Drew-Chris – Undisclosed Location

Over the next hour we checked his camera (sunrise only, nice pictures) talked about how he was used to ignoring signs and doing what he wanted (big star there but dangerous where we were), about his brother who was majoring in Engineering at Ohio State (he called it pre-business) and we got a bunch of pictures with him. Nice guy, very funny. He and his cast didn't have to do USO shows halfway around the world but he did it to support the troops, we appreciated it.

In February of 2002 I came home for the second time. I was relieved by; you guessed it, Chris Ham. I was proud of what we did but unsure of why we were still there. I really think we should have pulled everybody out.

I had long hair, a full beard and a one-way ticket from the Middle East (we flew out of Saudi) and security worldwide was at a heightened state. I got stopped and searched at every stop on the flight. I was OK and glad to be home but just a little screwed up in the head. I called Chris at the first hotel on the sat-phone to let him know I was back. I had a glass of diet coke (with ice) and a flushing toilet. I flushed it many of time during our conversation just to show off. It is funny what can make you happy, ice and a flushing toilet works for me.

We got metals, we got patted on the back and we got fired. We did what the Army wanted and we performed flawlessly and we played by the rules but that was not what the customer wanted, politics got me again.

As soon as we returned, two things happened:

1. We got fired from BCPO
2. We got called to Washington D.C. for another job (one door closes another opens).

Chapter Eleven

Soon after Chris and I got back from our contribution to Operation Enduring Freedom several things happened. First we got fired. We followed the orders passed down by command. That's what soldiers do, that's what we did. Our civilian government boss was pissed. He wanted us to do what he said, even if it went against the orders we were given, even if it broke federal laws. We wouldn't, and we got fired.

It closed one door but opened others. One was to the Rapid Equipping Force and Col Bruce Jette. Good guy, solid, smart and was awarded a Bronze Star in OEF. Many high-ranking Army officers are little more than politicians, just kissing butt and trying to get their next promotion. Not Col. Jette, he cared about the troops and he wanted them to have the best equipment available to fight the war. We met in Washington D.C. at his request. He had read a paper I wrote and was intrigued. First words out of his mouth I will never forget: "Boys," He said looking right into our eyes "my soldiers are dying." The enemy had stockpiles of artillery rounds and cheap blasting caps to set them off. They first wired the devices and burring the wires, used a battery to set them off. It was risky because we were watching for any activity like that and would often catch them in the act.

Lately the enemy had begun to use wireless detonators. They could wait until the road was cleared and then drive up to a trash pile and drop of a wireless bomb (later called Improvised Explosive Devices or IEDs) and a triggerman. When the convoy came by the device was detonated and soldiers died. We took on the task and I started the wheels into motion before we left the building.

Got our target set, controller, modulator, transmitter and really cool wide band small antenna together and presented a working prototype attached to the top of my 2003 Ford F250 pickup in three days. We even made a target bomb (with a light to indicate it was set off instead of explosive). It worked, it worked really well. We called it SSVJ. We delivered the first 14 in six weeks to 10th Mountain out of Ft. Drum NY as they were deploying. I built a new building and hired a crew to make thousands Even bought a shake and bake machine so we could test them on-site, make sure they would work in the harsh environment.

This is the part of the story where I start talking about engineering stuff because I am really proud of the design and how well my guys worked on this project. If you really hate this stuff skip forward.

If you are in an aircraft and want to sneak up on your enemy you can't always fly under the radar (sorry Top Gun). Sometimes the radars are on towers or mountaintops so they can see you for a long way. So we use Electronic Warfare to effectively make the radar units blind. And there are a couple different ways to do this. The most typical is a Stand Off Jammer (SOJ). You fill a KC-135 with EW gear and stand off beyond the maximum range of the system(s) you are jamming and transmit a signal that will either make the radar blind (high power) or unable to see (special modulations). All of the bombers and fighters can then fly in under the cover of the SOJ signal and blow up the radars and missile sites.

Sometimes you just want to fly in as small as a single aircraft. In that case you need what is called a Self Screening Jammer (one per aircraft).

The next issue is what kind of jamming signal do you use. A continuous signal is great but several modern Air Defense Artillery (ADA) systems have track-on-jam features so they can just launch a missile and track the continuous jammer. If you are within range, you get blown up. So we want to go with a responsive jammer. These can detect the radar signal and provide pre-programmed responses that can confuse the radar receiver and make them think you are at a different range than you are. I love jamming radars, radar guys hate EW guys, we don't care.

Now that you are an expert in aircraft jamming remember, responsive jamming good, brute force bad.

Now let's apply our situation to a vehicle. First some brainwaves decided to make it a stand off jammer, make one big, powerful jammer to cover the entire convoy. Bad idea. The convoy may have to go through a town or village and the buildings would block the jamming signal. Just like when you lose cell coverage in your car. Many of the bad guys are smart and even educated in our colleges and universities, they can figure this out and detonate the bomb when coverage is blocked.

And now let's address responsive jamming. Most aircraft are many miles out from the radar system when the signal they want to jam is first encountered. There is lots of time to receive the transmitted signal, process it to determine the best response and retransmit a jamming signal to defeat the radar system. When we are in HMMWV (new Army jeeps) and drive by a bomb, a triggerman presses a button on their transmitter (cell phone, RC car controller, garage door remote, cordless phone or similar) and transmits a signal to the bomb's receiver which sets it off the bomb. There is just no time for a responsive system to work, the jammer must be on all the time to be effective. I have argued this point with a great many who do not understand the problem (known as morons). So many morons, so little time.

So my conclusion was simple, a small jammer on every vehicle, and have them on all the time but only on target signals. So you got to know what the targets are today and be able to reprogram in order to address targets of tomorrow.

We built them, built targets, started production and a test program. Then we got shut down. Why you ask, I don't know but have been told some three star general could not believe that a bunch of cowboys from New Mexico could produce, in a few weeks, what his gold plated, high dollar contractors could not build in several years with hundreds of millions of dollars. This ass-hat shut down production and started testing us every way they could. They tried to show their systems worked and ours did not. They could not. Col Jette went to bat for the system (he knew it worked, it had already been combat proven) but when a Col goes against a Three Star general, the Col soon retires and the Three Star wins. We still made a few thousand systems and saved some lives but our production was basically stopped.

Every Monday I would get a report on casualties and injuries caused by IEDs, casualties and injuries that could have been prevented. Most of my guys would avoid me on

Mondays. The prologue of this book is based on an actual incident. I wanted to name the system after the Army EOD Staff Sergeant killed in this incident. Army said no. Many hundreds of service members were killed and many more were disabled due to home made wireless bombs (IEDs). Most of those deaths and injuries were preventable. The cost of an SSVJ unit at the time was $8500 each and included all installation hardware, cables and an antenna that was both highly effective and stealth. I hope the general who made bad decisions got a great paying job when he retired (mostly based on decisions made while on duty). When you sell your soul, you should get a good return. The next cheapest was over 100K, did not come with cables or an antenna and didn't work.

I spent the next two years in Washington D.C. trying to get the program turned back on. One senator even offered to help for a $50,000 cash bribe (through an intermediary of course). We did not accept the offer; most politicians are self-serving crooks.

I did not do well in the many meetings that followed. And got to be known as "The Beast" in DC circles. The process crushed my spirit. I had a hard time sitting through meetings with career officers that talked like recruiting videos but really were just politicians, kissing the right butts to insure their next promotion and guaranteeing a cushy job with some defense contractor when they retired.

Most could care less about soldiers in the field, they weren't there and they didn't care. I had no respect for them, no longer trusted the system and it showed. I had several long talks with my business partner Chris Ham and eventually stepped down as CEO of TMC Design.

I stayed on as Chairman of the Board. After Chris took over as CEO he grew the company into one of the largest engineering and manufacturing companies in the southwest. I retained 50% ownership but basically stayed out of his way, designing antennas if they were difficult and ensuring the main contributors for TMC were rewarded with bonuses and company cars.

We sold the company in December of 2020. I lost my clearance the week after selling the company, really a smart move on the part of the accruing company (Air Force Officers, what would you expect), I designed most of their systems but I no longer design EW systems. I still design and build Antennas. I don't work for ass hats, but I do make movies!

Chapter Twelve

The Peoples› Recording Company

In early 2008, I was approached by the Mesilla Valley Economic Development Association (MEVIDA) and asked "What can we do to bring in more jobs into Southern New Mexico?"

My answer surprised them: "Make movies."

My son was in the film program at the Dona Ana Branch of NMSU at the time. They needed to make a new commercial for their automotive program but their shop and classrooms were undergoing a major remodel that summer and not available for filming. I am a classic car and hot rod fanatic and had a shop with a lift so agreed to allow them to shoot the commercial in my shop (if I could watch). It was the coolest operation I had ever seen. Just like a military operation but nobody is shooting at you.

So when MEVIDA asked, "how could we bring more jobs?" My answer was easy. TMC already employed lots of engineers, engineering COOP students, machinists and fabricators but if you were in the arts programs you still had to leave Las Cruces to get a job after graduation. The young woman who starred in the commercial at my shop is a prime example. She graduated but could not find a job in the area, but needed to stay here. After trying everything including many free (or nearly free) student, amateur or low/zero budget local productions, she eventually started working at a convenience store mostly selling beer and gas. Nothing wrong with that, you do what you have to do, but she could have saved a bunch of money and time by taking that job right out of high school and skipped the expensive film education.

We had meetings for two years in my boardroom at TMC (I was still the CEO). We ate dozens of bagels and drank gallons of coffee and juice. We toured a multitude of locations for a studio and back-lot location and agreed on a lot at the West Mesa Industrial Park (owned by the city of Las Cruces) but never moved forward. We talked and talked and talked but just never moved forward. Nobody wanted to commit, in the end we accomplished nothing.

After two years, I realized these guys were talkers, not doers. So, with my son and another super creative guy Aron Hethcox, we formed The People's Recording Company, LLC to make a couple of short films. My film education started on day one.

What's in a name? At one point we had received an offer to buy TMC and I needed to consider what I would do after selling the company. I always liked and built classic cars, hot rods and race cars (I raced dirt cars, mostly limited late models for about 10 years). So I opened a company called Pop's Rod and Custom to build and restore classic cars then sell them. Well I was pretty good at buying classic cars and the restoration part, but when it comes to selling cars, I have no talent. I would have $8K in a car and some guy would offer me $5K for it and I would chase him off. No patience and a low tolerance for assholes and stupid people. My career as a car salesman was short.

Then we started a band. One of my nephews, Jeff, is a gifted guitar player, Troy Jr. is an accomplished drummer (multiple punk/rock bands) and I kind of play bass. I also got elected to sing (badly). I already had hats and shirts made up so the name of the band became Pop's Rod and Custom. We did a bunch of gigs, had a lot of fun and recorded 3 CD's but my Nephew got transferred to Iraq (he was also an Army Officer) and that was kind of the end of our band.

When we opened the film company it started as the People's Recording Company (still PRC, because of the hats). Our first real work was for TMC making a training video then for the Army doing some cool videos for AUSA (their year end conference in D.C.). Some time after we did a very cool and moving video for the Green Beret Foundation for my buddy Bruce (who was heavily involved in the foundation). The video came out great but when the closing credits rolled and Bruce saw the Peoples Recording Company logo with our sickle and boom mic he said "If you show that to this conservative group of folks they will all walk out and not make a single donation".

Early PRC Logo

He was right, the Army was not crazy about our logo either. It was supposed to be 'tongue in cheek' not a political statement, so we became PRC Productions (and still are today). The Green Beret Foundation did great (they raised nearly a million dollars that night of the first showing) but we did learn a valuable lesson.

Our first film was going to be *CHIMERA* by Aron Hethcox. Good dude, talented musician, we got to work but ran into problems, one actor wasn't available. We switched gears and made *LAST NIGHT ON MARS* first.

LAST NIGHT ON MARS by Troy Scoughton, Jr. also a good dude, talented musician and would become the best cinematographer I would ever know (shot most of our films).

LAST NIGHT ON MARS -

Last Night on Mars is a surreal tale of the supernatural. Alone in a dark house we find terror at every corner. Is it all in our head or something much, much darker...? Sometimes the things that go bump in the night are more than just our imagination.

You can see LAST NIGHT ON MARS in the first LADY BELLEDONA Film.

It was an expensive, exhaustive, learning experience but we were building not just a new business but also a new business area. *Shot Chimera Version 2,* (later renamed *QUIMERA*) using Aron's Girlfriend as the lead actor. Never allow that. Learned some valuable lessons, lost one business partner but made a couple of short movies (Aron opened his own business). Troy Jr. and I pushed forward with PRC Productions.

> ***QUIMERA*** *-A dysfunctional team of mercenaries takes on a mission to hunt a creature that they're not even sure exists. Secrets are unearthed, and they soon find themselves fighting for their lives and questioning each other (on YouTube).*

I tried to make a deal to include *QUIMERA* in our anthology series *LADY BELLADONNA II.* Could not make the deal work. Funny really, I financed and worked on the film but in the end it was more trouble that it was worth to include my own film in my own anthology. Egos are powerful enemies to success.

FILM Lesson One -

Short films are worth $0. Some refer to them as a calling card. They may be fun projects to make while in school but have no place in the market, so don't make short films and don't let the director hire his girlfriend as the lead.

Television was my next idea. I rented a couple of buildings and we built a small television studio and bought a bunch of studio equipment. All of the broadcast television at that time was from El Paso Texas, we were in Las Cruces, New Mexico and close enough to receive their signal (about 45 miles) but it was not local. My grand idea was to have a true local television station and I started making content.

We were recording VIVA LAS CRUCES every week and a couple of other programs and wanted to do local news and sports. I aired our content on the local public access channel, which reached about half of the population but we just could not get enough advertising dollars.

VIVA Las Cruces Poster

I even started a documentary series called *PLATICAS* (means conversations in Spanish) filming historically significant local folks that had a message.

The city promised to fund *PLATICAS* for 2 years (24 episodes) if we formed a non-profit. The Mesquite Historic Preservation Society was born for this purpose. The City of Las Cruces then reneged on the offer claiming it violated the Anti-Donation clause. It seems their rules and regulations prevented them from funding any non-profit. They would later fund another non-profit called *Film Las Cruces*, but I'm getting ahead of myself.

We made a film critic and review program called *TAKE TWO WITH TERRENCE*. The program was cool (Terrance was a super talented critic and I got to play a James Bond like bad guy and get shot by Terrance and his James Bond Girl and star of Viva Las Cruces, Consuelo).

BEHIND THE CURTAIN, which was a theater review program but the guy that signed up to be the host dropped out at the last second (literally the first day of shooting) and guess who got to be the host - me.

We got no support for local television from the City, although they did open their own television production facility and tried to hire some of my people, thanks for the show of support City of Las Cruces. We were also not able to generate any local businesses support in the form of commercials. I mean we did a few commercials but never enough to fund the effort.

We did several live broadcasts and on-location programs including High Heels for High Hope, the Las Cruces Chile Drop and even some local political debates even made two seasons of PLATICAS (on PBS and now on Amazon Prime) but as much as I liked doing television and wanted the local television project to work it just never did No local support means no local television. I still have a collection of cameras, tripods, sound gear and lights for a television studio but will not make that mistake again. Before you ask, no you cannot have the equipment and no I will not video your local church services.

FILM Lesson Two - Two fold

1. If you want to do local television you better have your advertising dollars aligned before you start and
2. Never trust the city of Las Cruces to follow through with anything they promise (more on this later).

So how, you ask, can a production company make any money? I'm not the guy to ask but I was not done yet, the goal was to make this a self-sustaining business. All the experts said "make feature films". It's easy, you just gather up all the local experts and write (or buy) a script and make a film, then sell it for a bunch of money and do it again, right.

First I needed to become a real producer. Anybody can claim to be a film producer. If you want to be a real producer you have to be in the Producers Guild of America (PGA). So I applied.

More on that is a bit.

*Our first feature was called **TRUTH** (l later changed to the **VIRUS**) written and directed by a former child actor who just happened to be a preacher. Shot it in a really cool location is Silver City, New Mexico (a closed hospital that we got full access to because it was haunted) great people in Silver, great location.*

Did our college campus scenes at Western New Mexico University – again, great location and great people to work with.

I had tried to get access to my alma mater NMSU but could not get a permit (still waiting). We had a name actor, Billy McNamara to be our lead.

I was the producer and had just been turned down (try one) on getting admitted to the Producers Guild of America (PGA). That was no simple feat because I had no PGA Producers to work under in our area (that's generally how it works). Took several years and several features (and lots of harassment by me), but I finally got admitted a few years later, I'm still a member today.

We finished shooting *TRUTH*, edited it, Aron and I did sound over Christmas and wrote and recorded the score and some original songs for it. We had premieres in both Silver City and Las Cruces. We made four web-isodes of background and released them. We even won a film festival in Buffalo, NY. We got some press and I thought we were doing everything right. Then we took it to the American Film Market (AFM) to sell (very cool place), everybody was there. If you're making films, or want to, it is the place to go.

After a couple of days Troy Jr. and I figured out nobody wanted our film. Not only did they not want to buy it, they didn't even want to see it or talk about it. All those great connections our former child actor turned director had, well, they did not really exist. He knew plenty of guys and had grown up there but was not a part of the club anymore.

Why? Well, it is a small club and this is typical. The film's budget was too small, our big actor was too small, the script sucks, not enough action, too much action, did not get into Sundance and not their idea. *OK.* No one had time for us (or our project) and basically wanted us out of their office as quickly as possible. We licked our wounds, scaled back, moved out of the television studio and regrouped. At that point I decided to start a distribution company.

FILM Lesson Three - Also two fold
1. Before you embark of a film project you might want to have a buyer lined up and
2. Most people, who claim to have connections in Hollywood, don't.

About this time we had a group that met in the Rio Grande Theater once a month called Film Las Cruces. We would discuss films, screen trailers and/or music videos and get together for collaborations and just to discuss film making in our area in general. It was free and set up by David Salcideo (who ran the Rio Grande at the time) , Dave Wheeler (Studio 603) and Bill McCamey (Las Cruces film liaison). I missed the first meeting but made just about every meeting after that. Every month we had lots of young people hoping to become actors, extras or just break into the film business. We also had lots of film students wanting to pursue a career in the film business.

We continued to make films and with the help of David and a new company, Borderlands Media started doing our own distribution. Look maybe you won't even break even but at least you still own your film. Over the next few years I produced a ton of films (I'll include a list) but in 2018 decided to go great guns and make more and bigger films.

RADIO SILENCE was our first film, shot in 2018 and mostly on a back lot in Radium Springs New Mexico.

We built a complete restaurant set and it withstood 50 mph winds from our spring windy season. I wrote and directed the film and we hired all local actors (mostly from El Paso, TX). Troy Jr. was DP and shot the film on 2K RED Cameras with Rokinon Prime Lenses.

THE DEAD OF NIGHT is a thriller with some horror aspects. We got some really great actors including Lance Hendrickson, Boots Sutherland and a bunch of great local actors. We also used the director's girlfriend and the lead (see Lesson 2-2).

The film was shot on 6K RED cameras with Cannon Prime Lens, on a location 25 miles north of Capitan New Mexico. This is a beautiful area and a beautifully shot film.

Troy and I argued a bit at first but he quickly found out I was right most of the time (OK that is a lie) and we learned to work together. I also broke my hip. You see I have a common problem called 20-60 disease. 20-year-old brain with a 60-year-old body. I tried to show some of the actors some Army maneuvers and as a result of that effort, limped around the rest of that year (often with a cane) into 2019.

RADIO SILENCE won a bunch of film festivals and we distributed it through Borderlands Media. Didn't make a ton of money but we owned it (still do).

We went with a LA film distribution company, VMI Worldwide, who had made significant claims in their ability to sell the film but did not meet one sales area in their estimate. Buffalo 8 (also LA) did the post and we hired a pro from LA to do the score. The distribution company (VMI Worldwide) cut the film from 120 minutes to 90 minutes, but I think they omitted many of the best scenes. In the end we lost our ass and don't own the film. I'm sure VMI will blame COVID, or that the film sucked, or that our stars were not big enough or that they were not in the film long enough but the fact is that they did not meet their projections, not even one, not even close.

FILM Lesson Four-

I bought the film back, recut it and renamed it Coalora Falls. It's currently making the festival circuit and won a bunch of awards in Paris. Spending a bunch of money on making a film, getting big actors and a LA based film Distribution Company guarantees nothing.

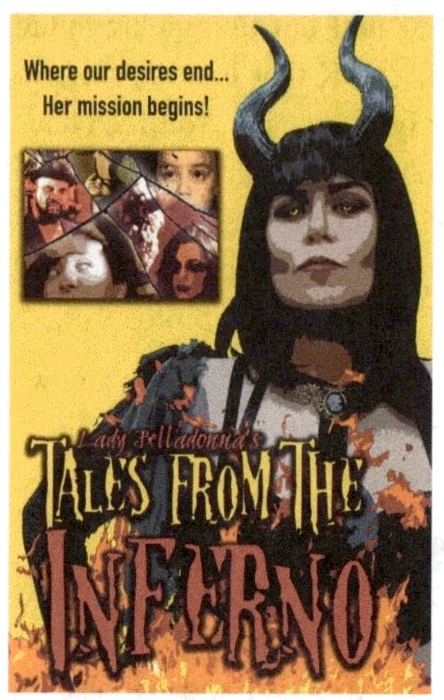

*We did a second **LADY BELLADONNA** anthology film and even had a short film contest to get the best short films for the film. The animation was really good and I think the fill (our part of the film) was also really good but the short films were so-so and it didn't do well. We had the premier at a film festival that was named the Borderlands Film Festival (no connection to us) and they sold out the small theater then had sound problems.*

Very amateur operation and I don't think they are still a festival.

For our fourth film of 2018, I funded an effort by Alexandra Zamora that was to be called *THE PINCHIE CODE II*. They shot the film on several locations in El Paso using our gear and some of our people. Because we were busy they were supposed to do the post for the film.

They missed their delivery date by several months and when pressed they delivered me the worst first cut I had ever seen. I believe any competent editor could have done this in less than a week and they had already charged me with 3 months. I fired them and tried to get all the releases and do our own cut but they would not release anything. I could sue but why, the film will have little or no value.

FILM Lesson Five -

Avoid doing business with amateurs or anyone on a first name basis with a bankruptcy lawyer.

They did get me to invest in a new western called *THE LAST SON*, or as I call it *THE LAST FILM*. It apparently suffered from the same ailments as our movie and none of the investment was ever returned.

FILM Lesson Six -

Do not invest in films. You will receive no return, Vegas offers better odds and you get free drinks.

Film Las Cruces (FLC) later became a non-profit, political organization with government and union funding. A New Mexico State Senator currently runs the organization with a film liaison handling day-to-day operations. FLC has attempted over the last few years to open several studios, make 'Big Films' in Las Cruces and even taken over a building (I own the adjacent property) to make a studio. It was a good idea but very poorly executed by amateurs. I tried to rent their airplane set (several times) but could not get a quote. I also tried to rent their studio space for a film but could not get a quote. ONLY BIG FILMS! Not some local flunky and you're an ass hole (OK they have a point there). I wonder how many other producers (who could be assholes as well) were in the same position and could not get a quote on using their facility. They failed and closed the building in late 2020, moved all their sets to the County fair grounds and probably sold most for pennies on the dollar. This was a great use of public resources.

————————— Plans for Buffalo 8 —————————

In October 2020, the building FLC was renting as their "studio" came up for sale. My plan was to buy the building, eject FLC and rebuild it as a functioning studio with three stages and a post-production house co-located in the studio. I teamed with some LA based film company (Bondit/Buffalo 8 under Matthew Helderman and Luke Taylor) and secured funding for the project. The plan was simple; buy the building, kick out FLC and rebuild three sound stages, in other words, open a real studio in Southern New Mexico.

I put together a proposal. We got it in front of the state for funding assistance and put in a bid on the building. Things looked promising and started moving forward – two months later someone else bought the building. My bid was too little and submitted too late.

We then moved the location to the West Mesa Industrial Park. This was a location we looked at several years before while exploring where to build a studio. We changed our proposal, got folks behind it again, and looked like we were gaining speed. And then several months later the effort stalled again. We could not get a quote from the city for the property. Yea I know it smells like politics again. FLC was not in charge so they shut it down. "If we can't be in charge, we will sink the project", this was and is their philosophy and it is a great philosophy for a non-profit. I figured out the problem (or maybe I smelled the rat) we were not ever going to get a quote on the property unless we involved FLC. I called them and sent them a copy of the proposal (they already had several copies but now it was official).

They informed my partners that the project could not move forward if I was involved, so I stepped out. A year later the Governor and FLC made an announcement that they would open a studio with 828 (another film production company) on Amador Avenue. I attended the ceremony. Lots of pictures, lots of speeches, some snide remarks made to me. Promises that the studio would be opened soon and the first film would be made before 2023.

Never happened and to date I have seen nothing to indicate it ever will. Film production in Las Cruces has dried up. I love Las Cruces but we have the ability to shoot ourselves in the foot with great accuracy and often. I do believe that FLC should now re-title their organization to a more correct No Film Las Cruces (NFLC), it is accurate and has a ring to it.

Which brings us to my last film lesson.

FILM Lesson Seven -

Stay out of the film business, if you can.

I need to explain this rule. My reason for entering the film business in the first place was to bring jobs to Southern New Mexico and West Texas. I honestly thought we could provide jobs to talented people in the arts like we had for talented engineers with TMC. We did make a bunch of films, documentaries, television, and I got to work with many very talented people. I will always cherish those experiences and that I got to be a part of that work.

You may ask *"Were any of the films, documentaries, and/or television good?"* I don't know! I liked them, maybe you will, and maybe not.

Did we make art? I can only give you examples.

We did a documentary called *SPIRIT RANCH* and I won an award for in a festival in LA. I thought that was a big deal but the really big deal occurred during filming.

The documentary was about equine (horse) therapy for soldiers with severe PTSD. I had experienced that first hand and then got talked into it by a friend who refused to take no for an answer, so we did it. During filming there was a former soldier that was severely hurt in combat and had just endured an hour-long car ride to get to the therapy session. He was not happy to be there. Then he had to sign release documents before we started, he was really not happy.

The way this works is that a horse will not come to you if you are angry. The horses were released in a large corral and the task was to put a bridle on them. Each soldier was given a bridle and assigned a horse. Our severely injured soldier was already mad and only got madder chasing his horse around the arena. After about an hour, the soldier finally decided to try the advice of the wonderful instructors and coaches present and calmed himself down. The horse came to him and he put on the bridle. It was a significant moment and we captured it. The wounded soldier was crying, my camera guy (Troy Jr.) was crying, and the director (me) may not have been, but only because I am a really tough guy and would never do that (OK, maybe a little). The soldier told us weeks later that after this experience whenever he was pissed at the world he would remember that day and could calm himself.

We shot our first feature, *TRUTH*, in the Silver City area and it was both frustrating (larger cast and crew, larger problems) and wonderful. We also did the post and I got to see the film come together and later recut the film myself later. Now called THE VIRUS. One scene when the main character is running across a field after escaping still gives me chills.

My first feature written and directed by me, *RADIO SILENCE*, was also tough and delayed so we ended up shooting in Southern New Mexico during late spring. We have 50 mph winds in Southern New Mexico during late spring. I remember my AD Robert Dean and myself cleaning off ½ inch of sand and dirt from the set before we could start shooting while the actors were in hair and makeup. The fact that the set did not blow down in those storms is a tribute to the builders (Frank and Michelle Powers, Gonzo, and my brother, Kirk).

During an opening scene after a long day of shooting (I broke my hip during this shoot) and trying to get actors to look and move like trained combat soldiers, my DP Troy Jr. (my son and one of the best) filmed the cast walking up a hill just as the light was going and it was beautiful, the best scene ever in my opinion, certainly the best in the film.

In another beautiful film, *THE DEAD OF NIGHT,* shot on a buffalo ranch 25 miles north of Capitan, NM it all came down to a look. This film was written and directed by Robert Dean and again shot by Troy Scoughton, Jr.

They were looking for a shot, I think it was the windmill shot and I was honestly getting a little tired of what was a long day, but they came across it and both knew they had found it. I saw the look in Robert's eye and looked over to Troy and he had that same look. They did not need to say a word, the look said it all, this was the shot they had been looking for all day. This is also a beautiful film, maybe the most beautiful film we have made to date. I will re-release this film later this year (2024) under the name Coalora Falls.

So did I succeed? Well it depends how you judge it. We made a bunch of films; we employed lots of people making those films, did post, animation, sound, and even equipment rentals. But by most business standards, we failed, we never made any money, never even broke even. So the business is not sustainable. I could blame lots of people for these failures but at the end of the day all of the decisions were mine. The film business is tough and filled with interesting characters. I heard today that Hollywood is the city of "crushed dreams". Spending money on movies is easy, but making money on films? Not so much.

Was it worth it? Well, we may have a studio in Southern New Mexico some day (I am rolling my eyes right now). We have made some cool movies here in late 2021 (mostly driven by Bondit Media Capital/Buffalo 8) and we still have many talented people here. We could do it but…we also have many politicians here that remain very good at shooting themselves (and everybody else) in the foot. I remain hopeful and have been talking to some of the far eastern counties outside of El Paso. Maybe we will go there.

I am also the film commissioner of Luna County now and trying to find funding to build a sound stage and backlot there just north of Deming (some people just never learn).

I am also planning to make a couple of films in the coming year, maybe a Sci-Fi film called Safe Haven Six. It's about the colonization of Mars. Might do some shorts in El Paso even if this violates my own film rules.

SAFE HAVEN SIX
What will you do to stay alive

Chapter Thirteen

Soon after the debacle of trying to sell TRUTH at AFM I came up with the idea of making our own distribution company. Troy Jr. had a friend who had just moved back to Las Cruces with recent experience, so how hard could it be. I contacted a friend of mine, David Salcido and asked him to throw in with us and make our own distribution company, soon to be named Borderlands Media.

The idea for this name came from an unlikely source, the leader of the NM IATSE union. He would make a yearly trip to Las Cruces and address the locals about film in New Mexico and what we should do to increase filmmaking in our half of the state. I believe these trips were mostly to appease the population who were investing state funds into an industry that paid benefits only to the Santa Fe and Albuquerque area.

The money being spent was state funds and Las Cruces is the second largest town in the state so we could have made it difficult if we didn't think it was a good idea to spend state funds on the film industry (in the form of tax breaks and incentives not only for making movies and television but also for studios). So once a year he would come down to speak to us and his message was clear, make yourselves unique. Sell what you have.

What we have is the borderlands. Three areas that are together yet all isolated from their governing bodies. Santa Fe is the capital of New Mexico. They collect the state taxes and distribute state funds as they see fit. Those funds generally go to Albuquerque and Santa Fe, very seldom south of Belin (I call it the great Belin Wall).

We get lots of lip service and very little actual investment. Who is to blame, we are. We sit still for it and continue to elect the same people to office who are more concerned with building their own name (and bank account) than representation of their people.

El Paso, Texas is right next-door but has the same relationship with Austin. It is a big city but I doubt they get the same attention as Dallas or Houston

Then there is Juarez, Mexico who has a relationship with Mexico City that is about the same. Together we are no longer three separate groups, we are the Borderlands, we are a unique and very desirable film location.

I believe most of Jon's talks were just trying to appease but he made a point (and I listened).

David, Troy, Jr. and I formed Borderlands Media.

We distributed a few films (mostly our own) and didn't make a lot of money but we got to keep the titles. Generally you make a film and sell it to some distribution company for 20 years, don't make crap and no longer own the title. An example of this is our first feature length film TRUTH.

The first cut was basically the director's cut.

Michael Cramer and Troy Scoughton Jr.'s **TRUTH** *starts with a premise that sounds familiar enough. The government has been engaging in covert experiments, combining viruses with nanotechnology to create the "ultimate truth serum" in its war against terror. The virus mutates, disaster strikes, and the black ops facility is shut down. Several years later, a group of students discovers the abandoned secret facility and decides to investigate.*

It sounds like the typical setup for a typical zombie movie. But this film, which has a limited release pending, is not a zombie movie. Instead, it takes things in a different direction (from Morgan on Media Review).

The film was OK, but didn't sell and most of the Hollywood types who saw it would not touch it. Why, you ask? Well, it was mostly written and directed by a preacher (Michael) and the message was clear: Christian good, Muslim bad. That may be the consensus by most Americans who have never traveled, but I don't believe that.

Don't get me wrong, I think there has been some terrible stuff done under the name of religion and God by all groups. There has also been some good. I further have had the benefit of meeting people of all religions all over the world and some of them were great folks, family orientated and just trying to get by like everybody else, just good folks.

Some were just assholes. It didn't have anything to do with their religion. Before you jump on a high horse and start yelling about 9-11 or some other act, I deployed and *you* probably did not. Yes some religious fanatics committed unspeakable acts but we have lots of religious fanatics right here at home.

As long as I am digging myself a hole here let me also say I do not believe in any difference between us. This includes all the normal reasons to pre judge including race, sexual orientation, gender, political orientation or if you hate my music and/or movies.

OK, I am lying– if you hate my movies or my music try making something yourself (and let me review it).

*So **TRUTH** needed some help. We had shot a bunch of Web episodes (webisodes) to help fill in the plot. I liked most of them (because I directed most of them) and decided to re-cut **TRUTH** using some of the webisodes and losing a bunch of the religious stuff. I called the film **THE VIRUS** and it still is one of our best sellers. If you don't have anything to do this afternoon, watch **TRUTH** and then watch **THE VIRUS** and tell me what you think.*

(Unless you hate both of them, then keep that to yourself).

Later that year, I met a really cool guy, Dave Noble, who was an Army Major stationed in El Paso at Ft. Bliss. We met at Comic Con in Las Cruces. He was also a filmmaker and he had made films at each of his duty stations.

When he was stationed in Louisiana, he made a film about a murderer in the bayou called Zydeco. Erin McCoy (Courtney Shay Young) and Rae Johnson (LaTasha Williams) travel deep into Central Louisiana, seeing when they soon become lost. The two are guided by a local merchant (William Hartley) to the town psychic (Rhonda Schaubert) for some unique local culture, but the visit turns dangerous immediately when they encounter the ZYDECO (Elgin Foster)! Don't ask what the BBQ sold at the race track was made of.

*Later in South Korea he filmed The Knight Squad Borderlands Media made a Grindhouse double feature on this one with **Nunja** (Autumn Gieb)*

*When Dave was stationed at Ft. Bliss (El Paso, TX) he made **Lost Padre Mine** and PRC Productions did the post production (editing, sound, etc.). Borderlands Media did distribution.*

Lost Padre Mine follows Wayne Braddock, a treasure hunter who, under the invitation of a member of the local clergy, arrives in El Paso to search for the missing Padre LaRue Spanish gold.

Lost Padre Mine is still available on multiple platforms including YouTube (from Buffalo 8), Amazon Prime and tubi. It is a good film and unlike many of ours is Kid Friendly.

Dave has just finished another production called Secret Within the Sphere. I haven't seen to entire film but I need to, maybe Borderlands Media can distribute

Airship Captain Verne Rudolph leads an adventure to acquire the Lelia sphere, an ancient energy course that the manipulative Victor Augustus will use to power his visionary city of the sky. Accompanied by the Duchess Adeline, Captain Rudolph finds him at odds against local law enforcement, air pirates, and many other adversaries determined to make the hero's life difficult.

Borderlands Media moving forward is now also involved in book publishing. A man we made a documentary with, Johnny Florez, wrote up his life's story on his deathbed and his close friend brought by his handwritten autobiography in a small spiral notebook. He wrote this over a span of time, and ultimately, on his deathbed.

His dream was to have it published one day. I of course agreed, how could I deny this heartwarming request?

I handed the tablet over to my grandson Conner, who had already been with our company (thus starting the Borderlands publishing team sector). It seemed like a simple task, however, the document was written in cursive and some of it was in Spanish, some with a dying pen… and over 18 chapters of it.

Conner did not know Spanish fluently, or 'dying pen', but over the next several months, with the help of some very close friends and family, he transcribed and translated the entire document.

——————— *Johnny Florez (In His Own Words)* ———————

Around this time, my daughter took over the publishing stuff. We used a larger-scale company to do the leg work. It was completely transcribed, in English, formatted, edited, pictures included, cover illustrations, etc. Basically, we turned in a finished book.

They provided the printing, some editing, and the ISBN. Long story short, publishing books with large companies, was very expensive. We didn't really profit from this book. It was a learning experience for us and overall a favor. However, it is still available on our website if your curiosity is calling!

One of our next big projects was based on a dream, and it's quite the wild ride! Instead of an autobiography, this is fiction. We have a little more freedom with fiction, as we get to paint the picture and describe the characters. Our author is a very talented writer, and we're excited to get her story out. This project is called "One World United", or OWU as our team refers to it.

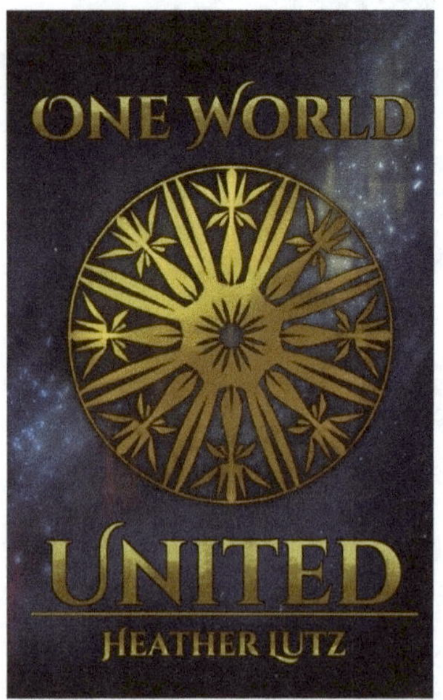

That's all for now, look for this title and it's sequel soon.

The publishing sector has been both rewarding and educational. It's something that we've all come to enjoy overall. With hopes of moving into printing as well, our business prospects are growing.

www.borderlandsmedia.com

Chapter Fourteen

So my business partner Chris Ham negotiated the sale of our company TMC Design for a tidy sum and we were good. Soon later I got a cease and desist letter because I was making antennas (for the purchasing company), not a great move. The non-compete was crammed in the middle of a bunch of forms that needed signing on the final day before acquisition. Would I have signed if I had read it? No. But money was no longer a problem.

Then my wife Sylvia got sick. She had been having problems with her left eye and it was blamed on a cataract or some blood inside her eye. One Doc mentioned a CT scan in the Albuquerque Eye clinic we were going to, but the head doc (real bitch here) said it was not a problem and even made my wife, a seasoned nurse, feel foolish for bringing it up.

A couple of weeks later we were in the emergency room because Sylvia thought she was having a stroke. The PA had a CT scan performed and immediately transferred her to the hospital in El Paso. They did a biopsy and found a lymphoma behind her left eye.

We made a trip to M.D. Anderson in Houston for evaluation. She started the treatment she needed. It took living in Houston for 6 months. We got an apartment, shaved our heads and I learned to drive in Houston traffic. I like the people of Houston and found it to be a very friendly place. But the people at M.D. Anderson; the doctors, nurses, technicians and staff, I loved them. They are truly the best in the world. They cured Sylvia and a year later she is still clear.

You quickly realize what is important, and for me, Sylvia is important. I even made red chile from scratch (no frozen there) for a super bowl party one of her nurses was having. Just love those guys. Made Thanksgiving dinner, Christmas dinner (well a couple of days later, she was getting treatment over Christmas) and New Years.

My son drove our car over and we filled the back with the stuff we acquired over the time we were there. We have been back three times for check-ups and in February of 2024 we went for our last quarterly check-up. I hope and pray it is negative as the others have been, truly a miracle.

So now we are at home and I'm working on a bunch of old cars (just got a '73 Chevelle SS), still making movies (well maybe), trying to build a sound stage in Luna County and finally getting ready to finish this book. I also built a shop and while wiring some lights and outlets, I fell off a ladder.

The moral of the story is life is short and filled with surprises. One day you're climbing the ladder and the next day you fall off and bust your butt (no breaks, just sore).

I still have a bunch of cool stuff to do in my life. Write a few stories, a couple of scripts, maybe a few films, a bunch of antennas, some hotrods; but mostly enjoying life with my lovely wife (yes her hair is coming back, mine too).

Troy and Sylvia Scoughton

Appendix 1

Film Credits

COALORA FALLS (2024 feature film, thriller) executive producer, producer, edit, sound edit.

THE LAST SON (2021 feature film, thriller) executive producer

THE DEAD OF NIGHT (2019 feature film, thriller), executive producer, producer

DA PINCHIE CODE II (2019 feature film comedy, horror) executive producer, producer

RADIO SILENCE (2018 feature film, sci fi, thriller) Executive producer, producer (p.g.a, mark), director, writer, edit.

LADY BELLADONNA'S TALES FROM THE INFERNO (2018, feature film, horror anthology) executive producer, producer

THE VIRUS (2017, feature film, sci-fi thriller), executive producer, producer (p.g.a. mark), line producer, editor, sound design and soundtrack creation/recording/mix.

LADY BELLADONNA'S NIGHT SHADES (2016, feature film, horror anthology), executive producer. producer. line producer, audio editor, soundtrack recording.

THE HEART OUTRIGHT (2016, feature film, drama), executive producer, sound edit/mixer.

DEVIL IN THE CITY OF CROSSES (2016, feature film, horror) executive producer, producer.

GOOD NIGHT SLEEP TIGHT (2015, feature film, horror) executive producer, producer, picture car coordinator.

TRUTH (2013/14, feature film, sci-fi thriller), executive producer, producer (p.g.a. mark), line producer, sound designer and soundtrack creation/recording.

DAY OF THE MUMMY (2014, feature film, horror) co-producer

EATERS (2014, feature film, horror) producer

FRANKENSEIN vs THE MUMMY (2014, feature film, horror) co-producer

CHIMERA (2010/11, short film. horror) executive producer, set designer, soundtrack recording/creation, props designer.

LAST NIGHT ON MARS (2010, short film. horror) executive producer, producer, sound recording, soundtrack recording/ creation, props/set

SPIRIT RANCH (2011, award winning documentary) producer, director, edit, sound recording, sound edit.

Appendix 2

Television Credits

PLATICAS (2010-present, historical documentary series, 30 total, 16 produced season 1, 14 produced season 2) producer, director, edit, sound recording/edit. PBS

VIVA LAS CRUCES (2012/13, weekly local television, variety, 29 episodes produced) producer, floor producer, edit

TAKE TWO (2012/13, weekly local television, movie review, 11 episodes produced) producer, floor producer, edit

BEHIND THE CURTAIN (2012, weekly local television, theater, 7 episodes produced) producer, floor producer, host

HIGH HEELS FOR HIGH HOPES (March of Dimes) (2012, 90 min. live variety show) video director, producer, edit